HARCOURT

Math

Practice Workbook

TEACHER EDITION
Grade 6

Harcourt

Orlando   Austin   Chicago   New York   Toronto   London   San Diego

Visit *The Learning Site!*
www.harcourtschool.com

ISBN 0-15-336486-6

2 3 4 5 6 7 8 9 10   073   10 09 08 07 06 05 04

CONTENTS

Place Value

Write the value of the underlined digit.

1. 4<u>5</u>7,932

_____50,000_____

2. 1,094,<u>8</u>23

_____800_____

3. <u>4</u>9,638,421

_____40,000,000_____

4. 390,<u>5</u>28,416

_____500,000_____

5. <u>6</u>,730,981,034

_____6,000,000,000_____

6. 9<u>3</u>4,870,139,562

_____30,000,000,000_____

Write the number in expanded form and in word form.

7. 124,570 100,000 + 20,000 + 4,000 + 500 + 70; one hundred twenty-four

thousand, five hundred seventy

8. 3,825,000,964 3,000,000,000 + 800,000,000 + 20,000,000 + 5,000,000

+ 900 + 60 + 4; three billion, eight hundred twenty-five million,

nine hundred sixty-four

9. 17,284,013 10,000,000 + 7,000,000 + 200,000 + 80,000 + 4,000 + 10 + 3;

seventeen million, two hundred eighty-four thousand, thirteen

Compare. Use < or > for each ◯.

10. 35 billion ⊘> 42 million

11. 2,547,912 ⊘< 2,547,921

12. 4 million ⊘> 500 thousand

13. 95,804,173 ⊘< 95,840,173

Write the numbers in order from least to greatest.

14. 342,019; 342,190; 342,109

_____342,019; 342,109; 342,190_____

15. 60,217,348; 60,712,348; 60,127,348

_____60,127,348; 60,217,348; 60,712,348_____

16. 5,455,505; 5,455,055; 5,445,595

_____5,445,595; 5,455,055; 5,455,505_____

17. 21,121; 22,211; 21,212; 22,221

_____21,121; 21,212; 22,211; 22,221_____

Mixed Review

18. $69 + 28$

_97_

19. 31×6

_186_

20. $96 \div 8$

_12_

21. $35 - 18$

_17_

22. $108 + 256$

_364_

23. 52×10

_520_

24. $500 - 190$

_310_

25. $180 \div 20$

_9_

Estimate with Whole Numbers

Vocabulary

1. When both factors in a multiplication problem are rounded up to

   estimate the product, the estimate is an _____overestimate_____.

2. When all addends are about the same, you can use _____clustering_____ to
   estimate their sum.

Estimate the sum or difference. Possible estimates are given.

3.	2,489	4.	398	5.	4,723	6.	7,132	7.	5,401
	1,601		415		+2,198		6,594		+9,188
	+2,109		+368		6,900		+7,301		14,600
	6,000		1,200				21,000		

8.	478	9.	263	10.	5,877	11.	8,528	12.	8,903
	− 26		−211		−5,318		−6,491		−4,575
	450		50		600		2,000		4,300

Estimate the product or quotient. Possible estimates are given.

13.	53	14.	76	15.	72	16.	47	17.	660
	× 8		× 9		×28		×53		× 42
	400		720		2,100		2,500		28,000

18.	371	19.	68	20.	480	21.	375	22.	824
	× 78		×37		×192		×591		×693
	32,000		2,800		100,000		240,000		560,000

23. $331 \div 5$ 24. $643 \div 9$ 25. $1,827 \div 59$ 26. $5,543 \div 77$

   70 _____   70 _____   30 _____   70 _____

27. $9,165 \div 28$ 28. $6,281 \div 875$ 29. $7,118 \div 614$ 30. $8,215 \div 897$

   300 _____   7 _____   12 _____   9 _____

Mixed Review

Write the number in expanded form.

31. 305,064

   _____300,000 + 5,000 + 60 + 4_____

32. 434,216,075

   _____400,000,000 + 30,000,000 +_____

   _____4,000,000 + 200,000 + 10,000 +_____

   _____6,000 + 70 + 5_____

© Harcourt

PW2 Practice

Addition and Subtraction

Find the sum or difference. Estimate to check. Possible estimates are given.

1. 504 + 343

_____800; 847_____

2. 684 + 193 + 217

_____1,100; 1,094_____

3. 3,991 − 953

_____3,000; 3,038_____

4. 4,616 + 1,382

_____6,000; 5,998_____

5. 4,183 − 2,851

_____1,000; 1,332_____

6. 794 + 578 + 909

_____2,300; 2,281_____

7. 17,079 − 8,805

_____8,000; 8,274_____

8. 29,114 − 13,513

_____15,000; 15,601_____

9.   12,379
      + 7,166
      19,000;
      19,545

10.   53,852
      + 15,098
      69,000;
      68,950

11.   60,118
      − 38,541
      20,000
      21,577

12.   43,192
      − 10,476
      30,000;
      32,716

13.   72,583
      + 16,205
      90,000;
      88,788

14.   68,450
      − 31,754
      40,000;
      36,696

15.   154,022
      − 46,389
      100,000;
      107,633

16.   864,191
      − 95,361
      800,000;
      768,830

17.   571,042
      − 462,790
      100,000;
      108,252

18.   389,077
      + 605,213
      1,000,000
      994,290

Solve.

19. 158 + 2,876 − 586

_____2,448_____

20. 1,422 + 806 + 539

_____2,767_____

21. 4,950 − 674 − 1,805

_____2,471_____

22. 70,376 − 5,845 − 3,541

_____60,990_____

23. 8,026 + 11,061 + 3,824

_____22,911_____

24. 1,753 + 2,210 − 1,907

_____2,056_____

25. 5,951 + 4,676 − 1,050 + 47,320

_____56,897_____

26. 19,321 − 1,322 + 939 − 3,084

_____15,854_____

Mixed Review

Estimate the product or quotient. Possible estimates are given.

27.   57
      × 26
      1,800

28.   685
      × 51
      35,000

29.   173
      × 96
      20,000

30.   915
      ×506
      450,000

31.   718
      ×386
      280,000

32. 8,161 ÷ 87

_____90_____

33. 3,307 ÷ 47

_____70_____

34. 7,985 ÷ 432

_____20_____

35. 25,641 ÷ 197

_____130_____

Multiplication and Division

Multiply or divide. Estimate to check. Possible estimates are given.

1. 46
    ×12
    500;
    552

2. 230
    × 15
    4,000;
    3,450

3. 417
    × 40
    16,000;
    16,680

4. 2,515
    ×   52
    150,000;
    130,780

5. 387
    × 66
    28,000;
    25,542

6. 217
    ×154
    40,000;
    33,418

7. 6,903
    × 627
    4,200,000;
    4,328,181

8. 582
    ×316
    180,000;
    183,912

9. 6,148
    × 744
    4,200,000;
    4,574,112

10. 8,132
    × 915
    7,200,000;
    7,440,780

11. 25; 24
    $4)\overline{96}$

12. 40; 47
    $9)\overline{423}$

13. 20; 19
    $19)\overline{361}$

14. 100; 108
    $7)\overline{756}$

15. 150; 14 r2
    $32)\overline{450}$

16. 170; 145
    $12)\overline{1,740}$

17. 50; 48
    $19)\overline{912}$

18. 250; 246
    $22)\overline{5,412}$

19. 160; 156
    $31)\overline{4,836}$

20. 300; 345
    $17)\overline{5,865}$

Divide. Write the remainder as a fraction.

21. $7\frac{1}{2}$
    $6)\overline{45}$

22. $39\frac{2}{7}$
    $14)\overline{550}$

23. $25\frac{1}{2}$
    $18)\overline{459}$

24. $322\frac{8}{41}$
    $41)\overline{13,210}$

25. $602\frac{3}{11}$
    $55)\overline{33,125}$

Mixed Review

Estimate the sum, difference, product, or quotient. Possible estimates are given.

26. 1,087
     2,109
    + 4,837
     8,000

27. 56,803
    − 31,942
     30,000

28. 347
    ×261
    90,000

29. 26,811 ÷ 885
    30

Solve by using addition and subtraction.

30. 9,271 − 3,587 − 1,266 − 2,650 _____ 1,768 _____

31. 2,114 + 739 + 4,799 + 557 + 1,632 _____ 9,841 _____

Problem Solving Strategy: Predict and Test

Solve by predicting and testing.

1. Ryan bought a total of 40 juice boxes. He bought 8 more boxes of apple juice than of grape juice. How many of each kind did he buy?

   _____24 apple juice, 16 grape juice_____

2. The perimeter of a rectangular garden is 56 ft. The length is 4 ft more than the width. What are the dimensions of the garden?

   _____$l = 16$ ft; $w = 12$ ft_____

3. The Hawks soccer team played a total of 24 games. They won 6 more games than they lost, and they tied 2 games. How many games did they win?

   _____14 games_____

4. Rico collected a total of 47 rocks. He gathered 5 more jagged rocks than smooth rocks. How many of each kind of rock did he collect?

   _____26 jagged rocks, 21 smooth rocks_____

5. Matt has earned $75. To buy a bicycle, he needs twice that amount plus $30. How much does the bicycle cost?

   _____$180_____

6. The perimeter of a rectangular lot is 190 ft. The width of the lot is 15 ft more than the length. What are the dimensions of the lot?

   _____$w = 55$ ft; $l = 40$ ft_____

7. The Wolverines swimming team won a total of 15 first- and second-place medals at their last swim meet. If they won 7 more first-place medals than second-place medals, how many first-place medals did they win?

   _____11 first-place medals_____

8. Valley High School's football team played a total of 16 games. They won twice as many games as they lost. If they tied one game, how many games did the team win?

   _____10 games_____

Mixed Review

Find the product or quotient. Estimate to check. Possible estimates are given.

9. 306×582

   _____180,000; 178,092_____

10. $8,246 \div 38$

    _____200; 217_____

11. $21,420 \div 51$

    _____400; 420_____

Tell whether the estimate is an *overestimate* or *underestimate*. Then show how the estimate was determined.

12. $1,872 + 4,774 \approx 7,000$ _____overestimate; 2,000 + 5,000_____

13. $321 \times 82 \approx 24,000$ _____underestimate; 300 × 80_____

© Harcourt

Algebra: Expressions

Vocabulary

Write the correct letter from Column 2.

Column 1

__a__ 1. a mathematical phrase that includes only numbers and operation symbols

__c__ 2. an expression that includes a variable

__b__ 3. a letter or symbol that stands for one or more numbers

Column 2

a. numerical expression

b. variable

c. algebraic expression

Write a numerical or algebraic expression for the word expression.

4. seven less than eleven

$11 - 7$

5. six more than a number, x

$x + 6$

6. 8 multiplied by m

$m \times 8$

7. 84 divided by 8

$84 \div 8$

Evaluate each expression.

8. 19×48

912

9. $63b$, for $b = 15$

945

10. $w + 178$, for $w = 226$

404

11. $a \div b$, for $a = 253$ and $b = 11$

23

12. $h + k - 84$, for $h = 46$ and $k = 73$

35

13. $r(s)$, for $r = 109$ and $s = 33$

3,597

Mixed Review

Multiply or divide.

14. $18 \overline{)1,854}$ → 103

15. $631 \times 55 = 34,705$

16. $490 \times 117 = 57,330$

17. $54 \overline{)11,988}$ → 222

18. Use the table at the right. If the pattern continues, how many laps in all will 8 swimmers swim on the fourth day?

96 laps

Each Swimmer's Training Schedule				
Day	1	2	3	4
Laps	6	8	10	☐

Algebra: Mental Math and Equations

Determine which of the given values is the solution of the equation.

1. $4d = 28$;
$d = 7, 8,$ or 9

_____ $d = 7$ _____

2. $50 - t = 28$;
$t = 20, 21,$ or 22

_____ $t = 22$ _____

3. $42 \div n = 6$;
$n = 5, 6,$ or 7

_____ $n = 7$ _____

4. $72 + v = 85$;
$v = 12, 13,$ or 14

_____ $v = 13$ _____

5. $m + 7 = 18$;
$m = 9, 10,$ or 11

_____ $m = 11$ _____

6. $s - 17 = 10$;
$s = 26, 27,$ or 28

_____ $s = 27$ _____

7. $c \div 8 = 3$;
$c = 22, 23,$ or 24

_____ $c = 24$ _____

8. $155 = 5k$;
$k = 30, 31,$ or 32

_____ $k = 31$ _____

9. $8 = 25 - x$;
$x = 17, 18,$ or 19

_____ $x = 17$ _____

Solve each equation by using mental math.

10. $e + 6 = 20$

_____ $e = 14$ _____

11. $x \div 2 = 10$

_____ $x = 20$ _____

12. $6 \times h = 300$

_____ $h = 50$ _____

13. $s - 18 = 40$

_____ $s = 58$ _____

14. $92 = b + 7$

_____ $b = 85$ _____

15. $90 \div t = 15$

_____ $t = 6$ _____

16. $m - 150 = 420$

_____ $m = 570$ _____

17. $8 \times n = 72$

_____ $n = 9$ _____

18. $f - 6 = 98$

_____ $f = 104$ _____

19. $c \times 4 = 40$

_____ $c = 10$ _____

20. $63 = d \times 7$

_____ $d = 9$ _____

21. $k + 28 = 32$

_____ $k = 4$ _____

22. $9x = 180$

_____ $x = 20$ _____

23. $6 = v - 58$

_____ $v = 64$ _____

24. $w \div 9 = 12$

_____ $w = 108$ _____

25. $p + 62 = 100$

_____ $p = 38$ _____

Mixed Review

Find the sum or difference. Estimate to check. Possible estimates are given.

26. 390
       $+ 789$
       $1,200;$
       $1,179$

27. $9,056$
       $- 1,732$
       $7,000;$
       $7,324$

28. $1,978$
       $+ 693$
       $2,700;$
       $2,671$

29. $47,813$
       $- 9,507$
       $40,000;$
       $38,306$

30. $73,681$
       $+ 50,342$
       $120,000;$
       $124,023$

Evaluate each expression.

31. $n + 701$, for
$n = 510$

_____ $1,211$ _____

32. $50p$, for $p = 53$

_____ $2,650$ _____

33. $r \times s$, for $r = 12$
and $s = 30$

_____ 360 _____

34. $h + g$, for $h = 65$
and $g = 41$

_____ 106 _____

Algebra: Properties

Name the property shown.

1. $67 + 41 = 41 + 67$
Commutative Property of Addition

2. $93 \times 1 = 93$
Identity Property of Multiplication

3. $4 \times (25 \times 9) = (4 \times 25) \times 9$
Associative Property of Multiplication

4. $8 \times (4 + 9) = (8 \times 4) + (8 \times 9)$
Distributive Property

5. $53 + 0 = 53$
Identity Property of Addition

6. $35 \times 87 = 87 \times 35$
Commutative Property of Multiplication

Find the value of n. Name the property used.

7. $6 \times (8 + 7) = (6 \times n) + (6 \times 7)$
$n = 8$; Distributive Property

8. $14 + (11 + 15) = (14 + n) + 15$
$n = 11$; Associative Property of Addition

9. $n \times 1 = 29$
$n = 29$; Identity Property of Multiplication

10. $22 \times 19 = 19 \times n$
$n = 22$; Commutative Property of Multiplication

Mixed Review

Write the value of the underlined digit.

11. $845,\underline{6}02,371$
_600,000_

12. $\underline{9}1,487,053$
_90,000,000_

13. $20\underline{3},894,312,906$
_3,000,000,000_

Compare. Write $<$ or $>$ for each ◯.

14. 31 billion $\;>\;$ 54 million

15. $637,945 \;<\; 639,745$

16. $9,574,018 \;<\; 9,574,081$

17. 2 million $\;<\;$ 3,000 thousand

18. $23,040 \;>\; 23,004$

19. $158,682 \;<\;$ 200 thousand

© Harcourt

Mental Math: Use the Properties

Vocabulary

Write the correct letter from Column 2.

Column 1

_b_ 1. Associative Property

_c_ 2. Commutative Property

_a_ 3. compensation

_e_ 4. Distributive Property

_d_ 5. Identity Property

Column 2

a. $58 + 72 = (58 + 2) + (72 - 2)$

b. $3 \times (2 \times 4) = (3 \times 2) \times 4$

c. $10 \times 23 = 23 \times 10$

d. $18 \times 1 = 18$

e. $6 \times 24 = 6 \times (20 + 4)$

Use mental math to find the value.

6. $37 + 14$ __51__

7. $65 - 23$ __42__

8. 18×6 __108__

9. $258 \div 3$ __86__

10. 18×22 __396__

11. $141 \div 3$ __47__

12. $78 - 45$ __33__

13. $49 + 14$ __63__

14. $41 + 18$ __59__

15. 19×11 __209__

16. $37 - 11$ __26__

17. $366 \div 6$ __61__

18. $320 \div 5$ __64__

19. $59 + 26$ __85__

20. $74 - 23$ __51__

21. 15×51 __765__

22. $88 - 54$ __34__

23. 43×21 __903__

24. $465 \div 15$ __31__

25. $56 + 15$ __71__

26. 15×48 __720__

27. $32 + 35$ __67__

28. $153 \div 9$ __17__

29. $96 - 25$ __71__

30. $37 + 14 + 43$ __94__

31. $(7 \times 12) + (7 \times 18)$ __210__

32. $5 \times 33 \times 6$ __990__

Mixed Review

Evaluate each expression for $a = 72$, $b = 28$, and $c = 8$.

33. $b \times 7$

34. $a + b + 362$

35. $a \div c$

36. $225 - a$

__196__

__462__

__9__

__153__

Solve each equation using mental math.

37. $n \times 8 = 56$

38. $19 + w = 36$

39. $h \div 20 = 35$

40. $98 - x = 59$

_n = 7_

_w = 17_

_h = 700_

_x = 39_

Exponents

Vocabulary

Complete using *exponent* or *base*.

1. A(n) _____exponent_____ shows how many times a number

   called the _____base_____ is used as a factor.

Write the equal factors. Then find the value.

2. 5^4 3. 10^5 4. 18^2

   $5 \times 5 \times 5 \times 5 = 625$ $10 \times 10 \times 10 \times 10 \times 10 = 100,000$ $18 \times 18 = 324$

5. 2^6 6. 15^1 7. 4^3

   $2 \times 2 \times 2 \times 2 \times 2 \times 2 = 64$ 15 $4 \times 4 \times 4 = 64$

Write in exponent form.

8. $1 \times 1 \times 1$ 9. $n \times n \times n \times n$ 10. $6 \times 6 \times 6 \times 6 \times 6$

   1^3 n^4 6^5

11. $10 \times 10 \times 10 \times 10$ 12. $y \times y$ 13. $4 \times 4 \times 4 \times 4 \times 4 \times 4$

   10^4 y^2 4^6

Express with an exponent and the given base.

14. 125, base 5   15. 256, base 4   16. 729, base 9

   5^3 4^4 9^3

17. 32, base 2   18. 81, base 3   19. 1,000,000, base 10

   2^5 3^4 10^6

Mixed Review

Use mental math to find the value.

20. $65 + 27$ 21. $20 \times 14 \times 5$ 22. $(9 \times 4) + (9 \times 6)$

   92 $1,400$ 90

23. $84 - 45$ 24. $3 \times 3 \times 3 \times 3$ 25. 7^2

   39 81 49

Order of Operations

Evaluate the expression.

1. $27 \div 3 + 1$

_____10_____

2. $(6 + 8) \times (9 - 8)$

_____14_____

3. $(6 + 7^2) \div 5 \times 2$

_____22_____

4. $(12 \div 2)^3 + (2^3 + 1^3)$

_____225_____

5. $(15 - 5)^2 - (4 \times 3)$

_____88_____

6. $(57 + 3) \times 2^4$

_____960_____

7. $(19 + 9) \div (2^3 - 1) + 20$

_____24_____

8. $(3 \times 7^2) - (5^3 - 9^2) + 10^2$

_____203_____

9. $3 \times (10^2 - 65) + (5^2 \times 2)$

_____155_____

10. $14 + (11 \times 5) - 4$

_____65_____

11. $12 \times 9 - 5 \times (15 \div 3)$

_____83_____

12. $21 - 15 + 2^3 \div 2$

_____10_____

13. $24 - (33 \div 11) \times 4 + 17$

_____29_____

14. $6^3 + 20 \div (14 - 9)$

_____220_____

15. $44 + 4^2 - (12 \div 2) \times 4$

_____36_____

Evaluate the expression for $s = 5$ and $t = 12$.

16. $50 \div s + 7$

_____17_____

17. $s^2 + 150$

_____175_____

18. $2 \times t - 18$

_____6_____

19. $(t^2 + s^2) - 3 \times 8$

_____145_____

20. $15 + t \div 6$

_____17_____

21. $(t^2 - 27) + 9 \times s$

_____162_____

Mixed Review

Use mental math to find the value.

22. 12×7

___84___

23. $37 + 62$

___99___

24. $434 \div 7$

___62___

25. $1,731 - 605$

___1,126___

Write in exponent form.

26. $8 \times 8 \times 8 \times 8$

_____8^4_____

27. $6 \times 6 \times 6 \times 6 \times 6$

_____6^5_____

28. $n \times n \times n \times n \times n$

_____n^5_____

Problem Solving Skill: Multistep Problems

Solve by breaking down each problem into single steps.

1. Louis bought a new bedroom set. He made a down payment of $200 and will make 24 monthly payments of $125 each. What is the total cost of the bedroom set?

_____ $3,200 _____

2. Copycat Printing charges $25 for the first 1,000 copies and $15 for each additional 1,000 copies. How much would you pay for 5,000 copies?

_____ $85 _____

3. The cash price of a mountain bike is $229. If you buy the bike on the installment plan, you must make a down payment of $50 and make 12 additional monthly payments of $21 each. How much do you save if you pay cash for the bike?

_____ $73 _____

4. Mrs. Gray's class of 28 students is going on a field trip to the aquarium. The cost is $4 for students who bring a lunch and $7.50 for students who want to eat in the cafeteria at the aquarium. How much money should Mrs. Gray collect if 13 students are bringing their own lunches?

_____ $164.50 _____

5. Mindy's car gets 27 miles per gallon of gas on the highway and 19 miles per gallon in the city. Last week she drove 243 miles on the highway and 95 miles in the city. How many gallons of gas did her car use?

_____ 14 gallons _____

6. The high school band concert was held outside. There were 25 rows of chairs with 24 chairs in each row. There were 327 adults and 141 children at the concert. How many chairs were **not** filled?

_____ 132 chairs _____

Mixed Review

Write each number in standard form.

7. 8^2

_____ 64 _____

8. 3^4

_____ 81 _____

9. 5^3

_____ 125 _____

10. 2^5

_____ 32 _____

Evaluate each expression.

11. $n + 12$ for $n = 8$

_____ 20 _____

12. $34 - c$ for $c = 15$

_____ 19 _____

13. $8y$ for $y = 7$

_____ 56 _____

14. $w - v$ for $w = 21$ and $v = 9$

_____ 12 _____

15. $a^2 + 11b$ for $a = 6$ and $b = 3$

_____ 69 _____

Name _____

Represent, Compare, and Order Decimals

Write the value of the underlined digit.

1. 485.03<u>6</u>

2. 16,005.8<u>4</u>5

3. 8,492.<u>7</u>792

   6 thousandths   _4 hundredths_   _7 tenths_

Write the number in expanded form.

4. 5.71   _5 + 0.7 + 0.01_

5. 85.083   _80 + 5 + 0.08 + 0.003_

6. 0.4625   _0.4 + 0.06 + 0.002 + 0.0005_

7. 17.00157   _10 + 7 + 0.001 + 0.0005 + 0.00007_

Compare the numbers. Write $<$, $>$, or $=$ in the $\bigcirc$.

8. 15.4 $\bigcirc>$ 14.5

9. 5.67 $\bigcirc<$ 5.76

10. 43.90 $\bigcirc=$ 43.9

11. 7.91 $\bigcirc<$ 9.17

12. 765.28 $\bigcirc>$ 762.58

13. 0.234 $\bigcirc<$ 2.304

Write the numbers in order from least to greatest.

14. 3,224; 2,432; 3,422

15. 88.5; 85.8; 58.8

16. 6.21; 6.02; 6.12

   _2,432; 3,224; 3,422_   _58.8; 85.8; 88.5_   _6.02; 6.12; 6.21_

Write the numbers in order from greatest to least.

17. 0.005; 0.500; 0.050

18. 317.8; 318.7; 371.8

19. 16.04; 14.6; 16.4

   _0.500; 0.050; 0.005_   _371.8; 318.7; 317.8_   _16.4; 16.04; 14.6_

Mixed Review

Evaluate each expression.

20. $4 + 3^3 \times 2 - (6 - 1)$

21. $(11 + 16) \div 3 + (4 - 2)^2$

22. $45 + (6^2 - 11) \times 2$

   _53_   _13_   _95_

Solve each equation by using mental math.

23. $m - 7 = 36$

24. $9x = 63$

25. $a \div 6 = 14$

   _m = 43_   _x = 7_   _a = 84_

Evaluate each expression for $a = 6$, $b = 120$, and $c = 54$.

26. $b + 295$

27. $93 - c$

28. $b \div a$

   _415_   _39_   _20_

Problem Solving Strategy: Make a Table

Solve the problem by making a table.

1. Earthquakes are measured using the Richter scale. The greater the number, the greater the magnitude (or strength). Some of the strongest earthquakes during the twentieth century had magnitudes of 7.2, 8.9, 8.4, 8.7, 8.3, 8.6, 7.7, and 8.1. The San Francisco earthquake of 1906 had the fifth highest magnitude of those given above. What was its magnitude on the Richter scale?

_____8.3_____

2. Late in 1999, one U.S. dollar was worth the following amounts in five other countries' money.

Australian dollar	1.5798
Brazilian real	1.8780
Canadian dollar	1.4796
German mark	1.9524
Swiss franc	1.5919

In which country could one U.S. dollar be exchanged for the greatest amount of that country's money?

_____Germany_____

3. Danny is doing library research on animals. He has spent 25 minutes reading about insects. He thinks he will need the same amount of time for each of 5 other types of animals. If he began at 9:45 A.M., at what time would he finish?

_____12:15 P.M._____

4. A theater is showing two films. The starting times for the first film are every even hour, beginning at noon. The starting times for the second film are every odd hour, beginning at 1:00 P.M. If the last show begins at 10:00 P.M., how many times do films begin?

_____11 times (1st: 6; 2nd: 5)_____

Use the table at the right for 5 and 6. The numbers are amounts of energy in quadrillion BTUs.

5. In which country is the difference between amount of energy produced and amount used the greatest?

_____United States_____

Country	Energy Produced	Energy Used
United States	66.68	82.19
Great Britain	9.23	9.68
China	30.18	29.22
Canada	14.36	10.97
India	6.94	8.51
Russia	45.66	32.72

6. In which country is the difference between amount of energy produced and amount used the least? _____Great Britain_____

Mixed Review

Use mental math to find the value.

7. 67 + 83 + 33

_____183_____

8. 449 − 398

_____51_____

9. 203 + 178 + 22

_____403_____

Write which operation you would do first.

10. 8 − 5 + 7

_____subtraction_____

11. 16 + 4 ÷ 2

_____division_____

12. (10 + 4) × 2

_____addition_____

Estimate with Decimals

Estimate. Possible estimates are given.

1. $3.8 + 7.9$

____12____

2. 7.1×6.2

____42____

3. $23.18 - 19.09$

____4____

4. $12.2 \div 5.9$

____2____

5. 4.09×6.18

____24____

6. $83.89 + 17.66$

____102____

7. $162.3 \div 15.7$

____10____

8. $31.6 - 8.82$

____23____

9. $7.7 + 118.2$

____126____

10. $101.2 - 34.9$

____66____

11. $\$35.99 - \$6.02$

____$30____

12. 19.8×21.3

____400____

13. $\$124.66 \times 3$

____$375____

14. $10.6 + 19.01$

____30____

15. 81.3×9.6

____800____

16. $810.1 - 69.9$

____740____

17. $602.5 + 87.3$

____690____

18. 397.9×21

____8,000____

19. $502.03 \div 4.9$

____100____

20. $\$88.20 + \$79.10$

____$170____

21. $1.8 + 2.9 + 11.8$

____17____

22. $\$203.99 \div 21$

____$10____

23. $\$199.50 - \$53.99$

____$145____

24. 8.8×7.1

____63____

25. $67.2 + 11.9 + 107.44$

____190____

26. $889.52 - 402.68$

____490____

Mixed Review

Write in exponent form.

27. $4 \times 4 \times 4$

____4^3____

28. $2 \times 2 \times 2 \times 2$

____2^4____

29. 6×6

____6^2____

30. $1 \times 1 \times 1 \times 1 \times 1$

____1^5____

31. $7 \times 7 \times 7 \times 7$

____7^4____

32. $8 \times 8 \times 8$

____8^3____

33. $9 \times 9 \times 9$

____9^3____

34. $3 \times 3 \times 3 \times 3$

____3^4____

Find the value.

35. 5^2

____25____

36. 2^5

____32____

37. 8^2

____64____

38. 1^4

____1____

Name _____

Decimals and Percents

Write the decimal and percent for the shaded part.

1.
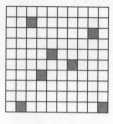
_____0.07, 7%_____

2.

_____0.60 or 0.6, 60%_____

3.

_____0.45, 45%_____

4.
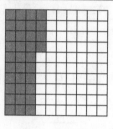
_____0.34, 34%_____

5.
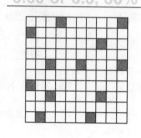
_____0.12, 12%_____

6.
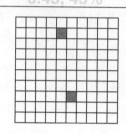
_____0.02, 2%_____

Write the corresponding decimal or percent.

7. 67%   8. 0.15   9. 0.92   10. 11%   11. 80%

___0.67___   ___15%___   ___92%___   ___0.11___   ___0.80 or 0.8___

12. 0.3   13. 64%   14. 88%   15. 0.14   16. 90%

___30%___   ___0.64___   ___0.88___   ___14%___   ___0.90 or 0.9___

17. 0.09   18. 34%   19. 0.75   20. 6%   21. 0.19

___9%___   ___0.34___   ___75%___   ___0.06___   ___19%___

Mixed Review

Evaluate the expression.

22. $6 + 3 \times 2$

___12___

23. $10 \div 2 - 1$

___4___

24. $16 - 4 \times 2$

___8___

25. $20 \times 2 + 1$

___41___

26. $(8 - 2) \times 3$

___18___

27. $15 \div 3 + 2$

___7___

28. $32 + 8 \div 2$

___36___

29. $20 + (6 \times 2)$

___32___

30. $45 \div (4 + 5)$

___5___

31. $(16 - 7)^2 \div 3$

___27___

32. $6^2 + 14 \div 2$

___43___

33. $12 \times (9 - 4)$

___60___

PW16   Practice

Name _____

Add and Subtract Decimals

Add or subtract. Estimate to check.

1. 0.34 + 8.19
_8.53_

2. 6.92 + 3.55
_10.47_

3. 0.418 + 1.291
_1.709_

4. 8.93 + 2.68
_11.61_

5. 8.7 − 4.2
_4.5_

6. 13.29 − 5.96
_7.33_

7. 5.41 − 1.36
_4.05_

8. 15.93 − 7.08
_8.85_

9. 9.328 + 1.294
_10.622_

10. 5.962 − 1.748
_4.214_

11. 4.036 − 2.751
_1.285_

12. 4.89 + 12.45
_17.34_

13. 8.116 − 3.094
_5.022_

14. 23.4 − 12.379
_11.021_

15. 20.68 + 7.12
_27.8_

16. 1.681 + 2.899
_4.58_

17. 41.783 − 29.822
_11.961_

18. 21.35 + 37.7 + 12.816
_71.866_

19. $245.62 − $109.99
_$135.63_

20. 41.6 + 27.56 + 16.942
_86.102_

21. 452.803 − 376.991
_75.812_

22. 111.22 + 77.5 + 83.947
_272.667_

23.
  446.09
  811.36
+ 73.52
_1,330.97_

24.
  8.71
  13.99
+ 67.2
_89.9_

25.
  89.01
− 67.56
_21.45_

26.
  25.8
− 17.226
_8.574_

27.
  23.75
  873.33
+ 2,586.02
_3,483.10_

28.
  71.043
− 58.649
_12.394_

29.
  36.583
− 16.007
_20.576_

30.
  3.056
  1,691.396
+ 44.21
_1,738.662_

Mixed Review

Write the numbers in order from greatest to least.

31. 21.10; 21.050; 21.8
_21.8; 21.10; 21.050_

32. 36.63; 36.33; 36.36
_36.63; 36.36; 36.33_

33. 5.912; 5.921; 5.192
_5.921; 5.912; 5.192_

Write the percent or decimal.

34. 0.98
_98%_

35. 73%
_0.73_

36. 44%
_0.44_

37. 0.06
_6%_

38. 90%
_0.90 or 0.9_

Name _____

Multiply Decimals

Tell the number of decimal places there will be in the product.

1. 6.3×0.75 **2.** 9.7×48.8 **3.** 5.96×62.15 **4.** 37.6×8.3

     __3__   __2__   __4__   __2__

5. 32.08×7.3 **6.** 428.9×5.6 **7.** 897.3×5.3 **8.** 186.472×9.6

     __3__   __2__   __2__   __4__

Place the decimal point in the product.

9. $6.17 \times 8.2 = 50594$ **10.** $24.01 \times 8.51 = 2043251$ **11.** $8.94 \times 5.27 = 471138$

     __50.594__   __204.3251__   __47.1138__

12. $8.04 \times 1.7 = 13668$ **13.** $19.6 \times 5.8 = 11368$ **14.** $30.7 \times 8.33 = 255731$

     __13.668__   __113.68__   __255.731__

Multiply. Estimate to check.

15. 5×0.9 **16.** 9×1.2 **17.** 4×3.47 **18.** $\$18.93 \times 7$

     __4.5__   __10.8__   __13.88__   __$132.51__

19. 5.55×9 **20.** 5×2.89 **21.** 31.82×4 **22.** 4.61×8

     __49.95__   __14.45__   __127.28__   __36.88__

23. 2.49×6 **24.** 35.98×6.3 **25.** 73.02×9.1 **26.** 8.5×16.03

     __14.94__   __226.674__   __664.482__   __136.255__

27. 3.91×6.22 **28.** 164.5×0.03 **29.** 28.14×1.52 **30.** 6.114×3.72

     __24.3202__   __4.935__   __42.7728__   __22.74408__

Mixed Review

Write the decimal and the percent for the shaded part.

31.
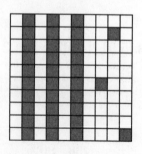

     __0.33, 33%__

32.
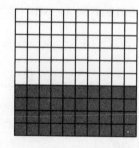

     __0.40 or 0.4, 40%__

33.
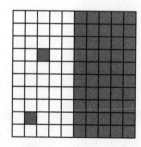

     __0.52, 52%__

© Harcourt

Name _____

Divide Decimals by Whole Numbers

Divide. Estimate to check.

1. 9)30.6   3.4

2. 4)9.52   2.38

3. 7)30.87   4.41

4. 6)197.4   32.9

5. 4)505.2   126.3

6. 5)$326.25 $65.25

7. 18)349.2   19.4

8. 32)172.8   5.4

9. 24)$299.76 $12.49

10. 17)6.8   0.4

11. 14)$7.42 $0.53

12. 35)23.45   0.67

Mixed Review

Compare. Write >, < or = in each ◯.

13. 0.64 < 0.68

14. 3.1 = 3.10

15. 0.07 > 0.008

16. 0.354 < 0.40

Multiply.

17. 8.4
× 6
50.4

18. 4.7
× 0.3
1.41

19. 219
× 0.5
109.5

20. 3.5
× 7.9
27.65

© Harcourt

Divide Decimals by Decimals

Rewrite the problem so that the divisor is a whole number.

1. $8.5 \div 2.3$ **2.** $6.4 \div 1.3$ **3.** $9.1 \div 0.15$ **4.** $33.17 \div 6.8$

_____$85 \div 23$_____   _____$64 \div 13$_____   _____$910 \div 15$_____   _____$331.7 \div 68$_____

Place the decimal point in the quotient.

5. $7.48 \div 0.25 = 2992$ **6.** $116.13 \div 4.2 = 2765$ **7.** $56.68 \div 0.08 = 7085$

_____29.92_____   _____27.65_____   _____708.5_____

Divide. Estimate to check.

8. $36.9 \div 0.3$ **9.** $22.4 \div 0.07$ **10.** $37.5 \div 0.5$ **11.** $89.6 \div 0.08$

_____123_____   _____320_____   _____75_____   _____$1,120$_____

12. $0.14\overline{)78.4}$ 560 **13.** $4.0\overline{)6.8}$ 1.7 **14.** $1.3\overline{)15.08}$ 11.6 **15.** $0.7\overline{)0.238}$ 0.34

16. $5.32 \div 0.7$ **17.** $1.88 \div 0.4$ **18.** $2.12 \div 0.2$ **19.** $5.4 \div 0.08$

_____7.6_____   _____4.7_____   _____10.6_____   _____67.5_____

20. $7.54\overline{)24.882}$ 3.3 **21.** $12.6\overline{)806.4}$ 64 **22.** $0.91\overline{)6.734}$ 7.4 **23.** $10.9\overline{)81.75}$ 7.5

24. $2.9\overline{)0.3335}$ 0.115 **25.** $0.18\overline{)64.296}$ 357.2 **26.** $12.3\overline{)84.87}$ 6.9 **27.** $8.7\overline{)53.244}$ 6.12

Mixed Review

Add, subtract, or multiply.

28. 78.94
      9.66
  $+ 103.71$
    192.31

29. $1,083.75$
  $-\ \ 706.9$
     376.85

30. 0.072
  $\times 0.48$
  0.03456

31. $215.6 + 49.87 + 8.351$ **32.** 42.83×1.91 **33.** $65.85 - 39.478$

_____273.821_____   _____81.8053_____   _____26.372_____

34. $430.62 - 288.74$ **35.** $192.6 + 847.56$ **36.** 17.335×8.26

_____141.88_____   _____$1,040.16$_____   _____143.1871_____

Problem Solving Skill: Interpret the Remainder

Solve the problem by interpreting the remainder.

1. Thirty-seven people are attending a party at a restaurant. In the banquet room, the restaurant staff has set up tables that can each seat 8 people. What is the least number of tables that the group will use?

_____5 tables_____

2. There are 23 pancakes on the griddle at a restaurant. The chef places 4 pancakes on each order. How many orders can the chef fill, and how many pancakes must be added to those remaining to make another order?

_____5 orders; 1 pancake_____

3. A library reading room contains a number of tables that can seat 4 people. What is the least number of tables needed to seat 54 people?

_____14 tables_____

4. A group of 5 friends wants to buy snacks. If each snack costs $0.75 and they have a total of $4.80 to spend, how many snacks can they buy?

_____6 snacks_____

5. The chef at a restaurant uses 3 eggs to make each omelet. If the chef has 200 eggs, how many 3-egg omelets can he make?

_____66 omelets_____

6. A total of 125 hamburgers were sold at a fund-raiser at the last football game. If the hamburger patties came in packages of 8, how many packages were opened?

_____16 packages_____

Mixed Review

Estimate the sum or difference. Possible estimates are given.

7.
$$671 \\ +902 \over 1,600$$

8.
$$478 \\ -310 \over 200$$

9.
$$831 \\ -289 \over 500$$

10.
$$1,226 \\ +533 \over 1,700$$

11.
$$661 \\ +2,403 \over 3,100$$

12.
$$1,729 \\ -494 \over 1,200$$

13.
$$488 \\ -391 \over 100$$

14.
$$2,994 \\ +1,258 \over 4,000$$

Solve each equation by using mental math.

15. $m + 12 = 15$

$m = 3$

16. $5w = 20$

$w = 4$

17. $x - 7 = 8$

$x = 15$

18. $q + 4 = 10 + 6$

$q = 12$

19. $6r = 24$

$r = 4$

20. $y - 9 = 10$

$y = 19$

21. $a - 2 = 8 + 6$

$a = 16$

22. $d + 3 = 21 - 7$

$d = 11$

Name _____

Algebra: Decimal Expressions and Equations

Evaluate each expression.

1. $t - 1.2$ for $t = 3$

1.8

2. $y + 4.6$ for $y = 2.4$

7

3. $8.2 - m$ for $m = 1.1$

7.1

4. $2.4 \div a$ for $a = 6$

0.4

5. $6g$ for $g = 1.5$

9

6. $j - 6.3$ for $j = 9.6$

3.3

7. $12.6 + r$ for $r = 4.4$

17

8. $4.5 \div p$ for $p = 9$

0.5

9. $7.24 - q$ for $q = 1.04$

6.20 or 6.2

10. $6.18 \div y$ for $y = 3$

2.06

11. $t + 4.66$ for $t = 2.1$

6.76

12. $5h$ for h $= 2.4$

12

Solve each equation by using mental math.

13. $w + 4.5 = 8$

$w = 3.5$

14. $\dfrac{k}{3} = 2.5$

$k = 7.5$

15. $1.4 = \dfrac{t}{2}$

$t = 2.8$

16. $m - 7.6 = 2.4$

$m = 10$

17. $3a = 6.9$

$a = 2.3$

18. $9c = 22.5$

$c = 2.5$

19. $3b = 6.4 + 2.6$

$b = 3$

20. $w + 10.3 = 21.7$

$w = 11.4$

21. $13.7 = d - 3.4$

$d = 17.1$

22. $4.8 = \dfrac{n}{4}$

$n = 19.2$

23 $\dfrac{x}{5} = 19.5$

$x = 97.5$

24. $7h = 15.4$

$h = 2.2$

Mixed Review

Estimate. Possible estimates are given.

25. $6.9 + 7.8$

15

26. 31.77×6

180

27. $63.85 \div 8$

8

28. $17.04 - 9.8$

7

29. $18.58 + 21.44$

40

30. 91.92×4

360

31. $54.3 - 19.7$

34

32. $80.8 \div 9.2$

9

Find the quotient.

33. $88.8 \div 6$

14.8

34. $59.4 \div 36$

1.65

35. $38.88 \div 7.2$

5.4

36. $31.108 \div 2.2$

14.14

PW22 Practice

© Harcourt

Samples

Tell whether you would survey the population or use a sample. Explain.

1. You want to know the type of computer, if any, that each student in your class has at home.

_____survey the population; There are not too many class_____

_____members to survey them all._____

2. You want to know the average number of siblings of all sixth grade students in your school district.

_____Possible answer: sample; There are too many_____

_____sixth graders to survey them all._____

Tell whether a random sample was chosen. Explain.

3. To determine the favorite sport of all the employees, Marcy is surveying the members of the company baseball team.

_____No, this is not a random sample; some employees are not on the com-_____

_____pany baseball team, so they will not have a chance of being selected._____

4. A company conducted an employee survey by interviewing 50 employees whose names were selected by being picked out of a box containing the names of all employees.

_____Yes, this is a random sample; all employees have an equal_____

_____chance of being chosen._____

5. Carlos wanted to find out which candidate the majority of his neighbors was supporting. He posted a notice at the neighborhood clubhouse asking people to call him with their opinions.

_____No, this is not a random sample; only people who see the notice_____

_____and feel strongly about the issues will bother to call Carlos._____

Mixed Review

Evaluate each expression.

6. $9.03 \div x$ for $x = 3$

_____3.01_____

7. $7m$ for $m = 2.2$

_____15.4_____

8. $4.5 - w$ for $w = 1.9$

_____2.6_____

9. $17.4 + h$ for $h = 5.9$

_____23.3_____

10. $k \div 2$ for $k = 6.4$

_____3.2_____

11. $6.58 + a$ for $a = 0.45$

_____7.03_____

Bias in Surveys

Vocabulary

Complete.

1. A sample is ____biased____ if individuals in the population are not represented in the sample.

Tell whether the sampling method is *biased* or *unbiased*. Explain.

The Tri-State Soccer League is conducting a survey to determine if the players want to change the style of soccer shirt.

2. Randomly survey all players who wear size large shirts.

____biased; excludes players____

____who wear other sizes____

3. Randomly survey all members of championship teams.

____biased; excludes members of____

____non-championship teams____

4. Randomly survey 80 players.

____unbiased; all players in the____

____league have an equal chance of____

____being selected____

5. Randomly survey all league coaches.

____biased; excludes all players____

_____

Tell whether the question is biased. Write *biased* or *unbiased*.

6. Do you feel that country music is better than all other types of music?

____biased____

7. What type of team sport do you enjoy playing?

____unbiased____

Mixed Review

Solve each equation by using mental math.

8. $w - 7.5 = 12.3$

____$w = 19.8$____

9. $5x = 16.5$

____$x = 3.3$____

10. $a + 6.9 = 14.3$

____$a = 7.4$____

Find the quotient.

11. $22.78 \div 6.7$

____3.4____

12. $49.6 \div 8$

____6.2____

13. $20.37 \div 3.5$

____5.82____

Solve .

14. Kyle rode his bicycle a total of 48 kilometers at a rate of 8 kilometers per hour. How long did he ride?

____6 hr____

15. Joanne earns $24.50 per hour as a construction worker. How much does she earn if she works 7.5 hours?

____$183.75____

Name _____

Frequency Tables and Line Plots

Vocabulary

1. A running total of the number of people surveyed is called

    _____ cumulative frequency _____.

2. A _____ frequency table _____ shows the total for each category or group in a set of data.

For 3–4, use the data in the chart at the right.

Students' Heights (cm)					
160	137	158	155	136	154
154	159	142	147	148	144
152	133	135	136	162	158
139	160	154	139	159	144
155	147	136	148	162	133

3. Find the range. _____ 29 _____

4. Make a line plot.

```
        X                                          X
X       X       X           X       X X       X X       X X X       X
X   X X X   X       X   X       X X       X   X X       X X X       X
+--+--+--+--+--+--+--+--+--+--+--+--+--+--+--+--+--+--+--+--+--+--+
133 135 137 139 141 143 145 147 149 151 153 155 157 159 161 162
                    Students' Heights (cm)
```

For 5–6, use the chart at the right.

Reading Test Scores				
98	100	81	92	78
75	96	78	84	100
82	100	100	86	78

5. Find the range. _____ 25 _____

6. Make a cumulative frequency table with 6 intervals.

Reading Test Scores		
Scores	Frequency	Cumulative Frequency
71–75	1	1
76–80	3	4
81–85	3	7
86–90	1	8
91–95	1	9
96–100	6	15

Mixed Review

Compare the numbers. Write >, <, or = for ●.

7. 31.7 ● 37.1 ____ < ____

8. 72.67 ● 72.670 ____ = ____

9. 66.61 ● 66.16 ____ > ____

Solve. Use the information in the table.

10. Estimate the combined population of the four cities. _____ about 240,000 _____

11. How many more people lived in Billings than in Missoula? _____ 32,794 _____

Population of the Four Largest Cities in Montana in 2000	
City	Population
Billings	89,847
Great Falls	56,690
Missoula	57,053
Butte-Silver Bow	34,606

Mean, Median, and Mode

Vocabulary

Write the correct letter from Column 2.

Column 1	Column 2
__b__ 1. mean	a. number that appears most often in a group of numbers
__c__ 2. median	b. sum of a group of numbers divided by the number of addends
__a__ 3. mode	c. middle number in a group of numbers arranged in order

Complete the table.

	Data	Mean	Median	Mode
4.	12, 15, 11, 15, 13, 10, 15	13	13	15
5.	68, 74, 71, 69, 74, 78, 70	72	71	74
6.	7.6, 6.2, 6.0, 6.2, 8.1, 6.7	6.8	6.45	6.2
7.	168, 212, 146, 195, 200, 156	179.5	181.5	(none)

For 8–10, use the table below.

Test	1	2	3	4	5	6
Score	91	84	96	89	93	84

8. Find the mean.

____89.5____

9. Find the median.

____90____

10. Find the mode.

____84____

Test Scores									
98	88	82	91	83	76	98	100	84	90

11. Use the data above to make a line plot. Use your line plot
to find the median and mode. Check students' plots; median: 89; mode: 98.

Mixed Review

Write the numbers in order from least to greatest.

12. 218.4, 284.1, 241.8, 214.8

____214.8, 218.4, 241.8, 284.1____

13. 6.17, 6.71, 6.107, 6.701

____6.107, 6.17, 6.701, 6.71____

Data and Conclusions

At Value Video, the number of days a video is rented determines the cost per day. The bar graph below shows the income from videos returned in one 24-hour period. The storeowner wants to know if lowering the cost per day encourages customers to keep videos for a longer period.

Days Rented	Cost per Day	Total Cost
1	$3.00	$3.00
2	$2.50	$5.00
3	$2.00	$6.00
4	$1.75	$7.00
5	$1.50	$7.50

DAILY VIDEO INCOME

For 1 and 2, use the table and bar graph.

1. How many videos were returned after being kept for 2 days?

   50 videos

2. How many videos were returned after being kept for 5 days?

   40 videos

3. Does a lower cost per day encourage customers to keep videos for a longer period?

   Possible answer: No; the store had the greatest income on videos kept

   for 3 or 4 days, but the greatest number of videos, 80, were returned

   after 1 day.

Two groups of students in Mrs. Brown's math class were surveyed about the number of hours they spent on math homework and studying math last week. The results are shown in the table.

Group A
2, 10, 4, 2, 4, 6, 3, 2, 15, 5
Group B
1, 5, 10, 1, 7, 11, 2, 1, 12, 7

4. Find the mean and median for each group.

   Group A: mean 5.3, median 4; Group B: mean 5.7, median 6

5. Which group of students do you think spent more time on homework and studying? Explain.

   Group B; The mean and median of Group B are greater than the mean
   and median of Group A.

Mixed Review

Find the value.

6. 3^3 ___27___

7. 2^6 ___64___

8. 7^0 ___1___

9. 5^4 ___625___

Name _____

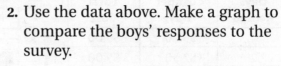

Problem Solving Strategy: Make a Graph

Patrice surveyed the students in 3 fifth-grade classes about their favorite fruit. These are the results:

Girls: apple–8, banana–12, orange–6, strawberry–13
Boys: apple–11, banana–9, orange–6, strawberry–10

1. Use the data above. Make a graph to compare the girls' responses to the survey.

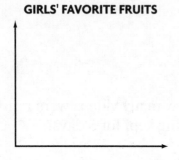

2. Use the data above. Make a graph to compare the boys' responses to the survey.

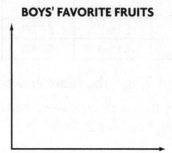

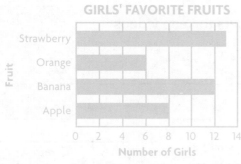

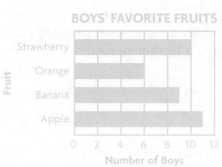

Choose the letter of the best answer.

3. How many more girls chose strawberries than chose oranges?

   A 1   C 5
   B 4   (D) 7

4. Which fruit is most popular with the boys?

   (F) apple   H orange
   G banana   J strawberry

5. Which fruit is least popular with the girls?

   A apple   (C) orange
   B banana   D strawberry

6. How many more boys chose bananas than chose oranges?

   F 5   (H) 3
   G 4   J 2

Mixed Review

Multiply.

7. 0.7×0.6

   0.42

8. 0.9×8.5

   7.65

9. 6.3×7.4

   46.62

10. 1.6×8.72

    13.952

Make and Analyze Graphs

Tell if you would use a bar, line, or circle graph to display the data.

1. the amounts of time you spend in your classes in one day

_____ circle or bar graph _____

2. the amounts of money you spend every day for two weeks

_____ line or bar graph _____

3. the number of students who play different musical instruments

_____ circle or bar graph _____

4. the weights of 8 different pets

_____ bar graph _____

5. **a.** Make a triple-bar graph of the homework data below.

HOMEWORK TIME

Name	Science	Math	History
Nigel	2.5 hr	0.5 hr	1.25 hr
Marty	1 hr	1.5 hr	0.75 hr
Julie	0.75 hr	2 hr	0.5 hr
Luis	1.25 hr	1 hr	1.25 hr

Check students' graphs.

6. **a.** Make a double-line graph of the temperature data below.

AVERAGE LOW TEMPERATURE

Month	Lakeside	Reston
Jan	20°F	12°F
Feb	15°F	18°F
Mar	23°F	20°F
Apr	28°F	25°F

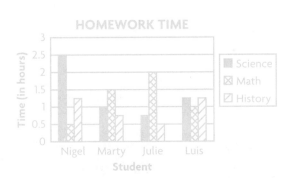

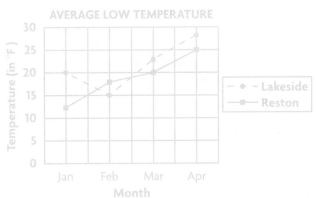

b. Which students spent more than half of their study time on one subject?

_____ Nigel and Julie _____

b. In which month did the greatest difference in average low temperatures occur?

_____ January _____

Mixed Review

Estimate. Possible estimates are given.

7. $71.3 + 68.6 + 69.7$

_____ 210 _____

8. $284.17 \div 7.24$

_____ 40 _____

9. 979.88×31.05

_____ 30,000 _____

Stem-and-Leaf Plots and Histograms

Tell whether a bar graph or a histogram is more appropriate.

1. number of fish caught at different times of day

2. average monthly phone bill for every month of one year

3. number of shoppers in a store during 3 different time intervals

_____ histogram _____   _____ bar graph _____   _____ histogram _____

Make a stem-and-leaf plot of each set of data.

4. Janet's math test scores:
   95, 83, 78, 91, 75, 85, 91, 98, 80

Janet's Math Test Scores

```
7 | 5   8
8 | 0   3   5    Key: 8|3 = 83
9 | 1   1   5   8
```

5. Raoul's golf scores:
   79, 85, 82, 86, 90, 94, 83, 85, 79, 91

Raoul's Golf Scores

```
7 | 9   9
8 | 2   3   5   5   6
9 | 0   1   4        Key: 9|0 = 90
```

For 6–7, use the table below.

Campers at Day Camp

Age	5–7	8–10	11–13	14–16
Number	6	11	18	9

6. Make a histogram. Check students' graphs.

7. How would the number of campers in each group change if you used 5 groups instead of 4 groups?

_____ The number of campers per _____

_____ group would decrease. _____

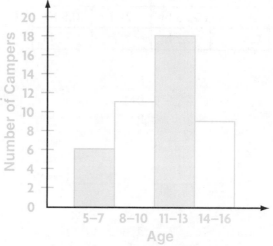

Campers at Day Camp

For 8–9, use the histogram at the right.

8. During which time period did the most flights arrive?

_____ 9:00–10:59 _____

9. How many flights arrived after 11:00?

_____ 7 flights _____

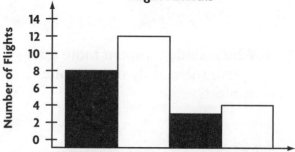

Flight Arrivals

Mixed Review

10. Bill has 180 baseball cards. He has 3 times as many infielders as outfielders. How many of each does he have?

_____ 135 infielders; 45 outfielders _____

11. Tim gave a clerk $20.00 for a book and received $3.85 in change. How much did the book cost?

_____ $16.15 _____

© Harcourt

Box-and-Whisker Graphs

For 1–3, use the box-and-whisker graph below.

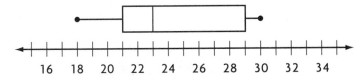

1. What is the median? _____23_____

2. What are the lower and upper quartiles? ____21; 29____

3. What are the lower and upper extremes and the range? ___18; 30; 12___

For 4–8, use the data in the chart below.

Lengths of Phone Calls (in min)									
17	21	16	22	24	26	18	28	25	29
21	18	14	23	25	18	26	24	22	23

4. What is the median? ___22.5___

5. What are the lower and upper quartiles? ____18; 25____

6. What are the lower and upper extremes and the range? ___14; 29; 15___

7. Make a box-and-whisker graph. Check students' graphs.

8. What fractional part of the data is less than 25 minutes? ____$\frac{7}{10}$____

Mixed Review

For 9–10, use the data in the chart above for 4–8.

9. Complete the cumulative frequency table below for the data.

Lengths of Phone Calls		
Minutes	Frequency	Cumulative Frequency
11–15	1	1
16–20	5	6
21–25	10	16
26–30	4	20

10. Make a stem-and-leaf plot for the data.

Lengths of Phone Calls	
Stem	Leaves
1	4 6 7 8 8 8
2	1 1 2 2 3 3 4 4 5 5 6 6 8 9

Misleading Graphs

Renee asked each student in her math class the following question: "Would you rather have some great vanilla ice cream or would you prefer chocolate or strawberry?"

For 1–2, use the graph at the right, which shows the results of her survey.

Strawberry 10%

Chocolate 25%

Vanilla 65%

1. Could the way Renee asked the question have influenced her classmates' answers? Explain.

   _____Yes. The question is biased and could_____

   _____lead people to choose vanilla ice cream._____

2. Tell how you could rewrite the question so it would not influence the results of the survey.

   _____Possible answer: "Which ice cream flavor do you_____

   _____prefer, chocolate, strawberry, or vanilla?"_____

A television network used the graph at the right. The network wanted to convince viewers that one of its shows, Show A, was far more popular than one of its competitors' shows, Show B, which airs at the same time.

Television Shows

Percent of Viewers

40
35
30
25
20
15
10

A   B
Shows

3. The bar for Show A is about how many times as high as the bar for Show B?

   _____about twice as high_____

4. Does twice the percent of the viewing audience watch

   Show A as watches Show B? _____no_____

5. How can you change the graph so that it is not misleading?

   _____Adjust the scale to start at zero and have equal intervals._____

Mixed Review

During one day at an airport, an airline experienced flight delays of the following numbers of minutes: 5, 7, 5, 10, 15, 15, 20, 23.

6. Find the mean length of all the flight delays. _____12.5 min_____

7. Find the median length of all the flight delays. _____12.5 min_____

Evaluate each expression.

8. $g + 1.7$ for $g = 3.3$ 9. $5y$ for $y = 1.8$ 10. $p - 4.9$ for $p = 11$

   _____5_____   _____9_____   _____6.1_____

© Harcourt

Name _____

Divisibility

Tell whether each number is divisible by 2, 3, 4, 5, 6, 8, 9, or 10.

1. 30

2, 3, 5, 6, 10

2. 24

2, 3, 4, 6, 8

3. 115

5

4. 240

2, 3, 4, 5, 6, 8, 10

5. 486

2, 3, 6, 9

6. 235

5

7. 279

3, 9

8. 801

3, 9

9. 145

5

10. 650

2, 5, 10

11. 736

2, 4, 8

12. 1,200

2, 3, 4, 5, 6, 8, 10

13. 207

3, 9

14. 723

3

15. 2,344

2, 4, 8

16. 868

2, 4

17. 694

2

18. 4,464

2, 3, 4, 6, 8, 9

19. 3,894

2, 3, 6

20. 306

2, 3, 6, 9

21. 836

2, 4

22. 5,962

2

23. 2,388

2, 3, 4, 6

24. 792

2, 3, 4, 6, 8, 9

25. 14,730

2, 3, 5, 6, 10

26. 24,456

2, 3, 4, 6, 8

27. 7,677

3, 9

28. 34,248

2, 3, 4, 6, 8

For 29–31, write *T* or *F* to tell whether each statement is true or false. If it is false, give an example that shows it is false.

29. No odd number is divisible by 2. ____T____

30. All numbers that are divisible by 4 are also divisible by 2. ____T____

31. All numbers that are divisible by 3 are also divisible by 6. ____F; 9____

32. A number is between 40 and 50 and is divisible by both 3 and 4.

What is the number? ____48____

Mixed Review

Add or subtract mentally.

33. 451 − 71

380

34. 898 − 196

702

35. 109 + 46 + 54

209

Prime and Composite Numbers

List the factors for each number. Write *prime* or *composite*.

1. 25

_____1, 5, 25; composite_____

_____

2. 41

_____1, 41; prime_____

_____

3. 48

_____1, 2, 3, 4, 6, 8, 12, 16,_____

_____24, 48; composite_____

4. 39

_____1, 3, 13, 39;_____

_____composite_____

5. 60

_____1, 2, 3, 4, 5, 6, 10, 12, 15,_____

_____20, 30, 60; composite_____

6. 34

_____1, 2, 17, 34;_____

_____composite_____

7. 59

_____1, 59; prime_____

_____

8. 42

_____1, 2, 3, 6, 7, 14, 21, 42;_____

_____composite_____

9. 35

_____1, 5, 7, 35; composite_____

_____

10. 56

_____1, 2, 4, 7, 8, 14, 28,_____

_____56; composite_____

11. 30

_____1, 2, 3, 5, 6, 10, 15, 30;_____

_____composite_____

12. 23

_____1, 23; prime_____

_____

13. 80

_____1, 2, 4, 5, 8, 10, 16,_____

_____20, 40, 80; composite_____

14. 67

_____1, 67; prime_____

_____

15. 104

_____1, 2, 4, 8, 13, 26, 52,_____

_____104; composite_____

Mixed Review

Find the mean of each of the following data sets.

16. 34, 41, 39, 26

_____35_____

17. 80, 90, 85, 80, 100

_____87_____

18. 3, 8, 6, 10, 5, 4, 7, 5

_____6_____

19. 124, 132, 180, 200

_____159_____

20. 29, 23, 40, 37, 26, 25

_____30_____

21. 1.3, 1.1, 2.1, 0.8, 0.7

_____1.2_____

Prime Factorization

Vocabulary

1. Write *true* or *false*. Prime factorization renames a composite

   number as the product of prime factors. _____true_____

Use division or a factor tree to find the prime factorization.

2. 28   3. 50   4. 76   5. 108

___2 × 2 × 7___   ___2 × 5 × 5___   ___2 × 2 × 19___   ___2×2×3×3×3___

6. 55   7. 120   8. 92

___5 × 11___   ___2 × 2 × 2 × 3 × 5___   ___2 × 2 × 23___

Write the prime factorization in exponent form.

9. 27   10. 100   11. 780

___3 × 3 × 3; 3^3___   ___2 × 2 × 5 × 5; $2^2 × 5^2$___   ___2 × 2 × 3 × 5 × 13;___

                                                  ___$2^2 × 3 × 5 × 13$___

Solve for *n* to complete the prime factorization.

12. $n \times 17 = 51$ ___n = 3___   13. $3^n \times 2 = 18$ ___n = 2___   14. $2 \times 2 \times 2 \times n = 40$ ___n = 5___

Mixed Review

For 15–18, find the mean, median, and mode.

15. 28, 35, 40, 28, 33, 36, 39, 31   16. 7, 7, 8, 9, 6, 6, 7, 10, 10, 9

_____33.75; 34; 28_____   _____7.9; 7.5; 7_____

17. 428, 472, 510, 386, 440   18. 78, 80, 95, 83, 100, 89, 88, 95

_____447.2; 440; no mode_____   _____88.5; 88.5; 95_____

19. There are 24 students in Mrs. Garcia's class. She wants to divide the
    class evenly into groups of at least 4 students. Write the ways in
    which she can divide the class.

_____2 groups of 12, 3 groups of 8,_____

_____4 groups of 6, or 6 groups of 4_____

Least Common Multiple and Greatest Common Factor

Vocabulary

Complete.

1. The smallest of the common multiples is called the

   _____ least common multiple, or LCM _____.

2. The largest of the common factors is called the

   _____ greatest common factor, or GCF _____.

List the first five multiples of each number.

3. 9   4. 14   5. 22

   _9, 18, 27, 36, 45_   _14, 28, 42, 56, 70_   _22, 44, 66, 88, 110_

Find the LCM of each set of numbers.

6. 12, 18   7. 7, 14   8. 16, 20   9. 4, 5, 6   10. 2, 6, 7

   _36_   _14_   _80_   _60_   _42_

Find the GCF of each set of numbers.

11. 15, 45   12. 6, 14   13. 24, 40   14. 8, 12, 52   15. 16, 24, 32

   _15_   _2_   _8_   _4_   _8_

Find a pair of numbers for each set of conditions.

16. The LCM is 35.   17. The LCM is 36   18. The LCM is 120.
    The GCF is 7.   The GCF is 1.   The GCF is 10.

   7 and 35   _4 and 9_   _30 and 40_

Mixed Review

Determine whether each number is divisible by 2, 3, 4, 5, 6, 8, 9, or 10.

19. 72 _____ 2, 3, 4, 6, 8, 9 _____   20. 80 _____ 2, 4, 5, 8, 10 _____

21. 324 _____ 2, 3, 4, 6, 9 _____   22. 1,500 _____ 2, 3, 4, 5, 6, 10 _____

Solve for n to complete the prime factorization.

23. $2 \times n \times 7 = 42$ _$n = 3$_   24. $3^2 \times n = 63$ _$n = 7$_   25. $5 \times 7 \times n = 385$ _$n = 11$_

Find the quotient.

26. $24.14 \div 7.1$ _3.4_   27. $17.29 \div 3.8$ _4.55_   28. $65.024 \div 6.35$ _10.24_

PW36 Practice

Problem Solving Strategy: Make an Organized List

Solve the problem by making an organized list.

1. Jack and Ashley begin jogging around a quarter-mile track at the same time. Ashley takes 2 minutes to complete each lap and Jack takes 3 minutes. How many laps will each have run the first time they are side-by-side again at the point where they began?

_____ Ashley: 3 laps; Jack: 2 laps _____

2. Terrence is taking two medications for his flu. He begins taking them both at 10:00 P.M. on Tuesday. If he takes one every 8 hours and the other every 10 hours, on what day and at what time will he take the two medications together again?

_____ 2:00 P.M. on Thursday _____

3. A large high school has a marching band with 64 woodwind players and 72 brass players. All members of the band line up in rows of equal size. Only musicians playing the same instruments are in each row. What is the greatest number of musicians who can be in one row?

_____ 8 musicians _____

4. Brice plays in a basketball league. In his last game, he scored more than 20 but fewer than 30 points by making a combination of 2- and 3-point shots. If he made 5 more 2-point shots than 3-point shots, how many of each type did he make?

_____ 8 2-point shots, 3 3-point shots _____

5. Aki is buying franks and buns for a field trip. She sees franks in packages of 6 and buns in packages of 8. There are 70 people going on the trip. What is the least number of each she can buy so there are franks and buns for everyone, with no extra packages?

_____ 9 packages of buns, _____

_____ 12 packages of franks _____

6. Kiona has 235 CDs. She is buying CD holders for her collection. The two types that she likes hold 20 CDs and 12 CDs each. She wants to buy the same number of each type. What is the least number of each type of CD holder that Kiona will have to buy to hold her entire CD collection?

_____ 8 of each type _____

Mixed Review

Estimate the sum or difference. Possible estimates are given.

7. $80 + 31 + 87$

_____ 200 _____

8. $710 - 189$

_____ 500 _____

9. $1,208 + 877 + 439$

_____ 2,500 _____

10. $7,151 - 2,993$

_____ 4,000 _____

11. $67 + 123 + 804$

_____ 1,000 _____

12. $920 - 592$

_____ 300 _____

Equivalent Fractions and Simplest Form

Vocabulary

Complete.

1. When the numerator and denominator of a fraction have no common

   factor other than 1, the fraction is in _____simplest form_____.

2. Fractions that name the same amount or the same part of a whole are called

   _____equivalent fractions_____.

Write the factors common to the numerator and denominator.

3. $\frac{8}{32}$ 4. $\frac{10}{50}$ 5. $\frac{2}{13}$ 6. $\frac{14}{49}$ 7. $\frac{1}{19}$

   1, 2, 4, 8   1, 2, 5, 10   1   1, 7   1

8. $\frac{12}{18}$ 9. $\frac{25}{75}$ 10. $\frac{15}{40}$ 11. $\frac{9}{54}$ 12. $\frac{6}{33}$

   1, 2, 3, 6   1, 5, 25   1, 5   1, 3, 9   1, 3

Write the fraction in simplest form.

13. $\frac{9}{36}$ $\frac{1}{4}$ 14. $\frac{15}{50}$ $\frac{3}{10}$ 15. $\frac{11}{121}$ $\frac{1}{11}$ 16. $\frac{15}{36}$ $\frac{5}{12}$ 17. $\frac{14}{28}$ $\frac{1}{2}$

18. $\frac{30}{66}$ $\frac{5}{11}$ 19. $\frac{63}{72}$ $\frac{7}{8}$ 20. $\frac{27}{81}$ $\frac{1}{3}$ 21. $\frac{25}{65}$ $\frac{5}{13}$ 22. $\frac{12}{42}$ $\frac{2}{7}$

Complete.

23. $\frac{36}{72} = \frac{1}{\boxed{2}}$ 24. $\frac{\boxed{50}}{75} = \frac{2}{3}$ 25. $\frac{17}{\boxed{85}} = \frac{1}{5}$ 26. $\frac{63}{84} = \frac{3}{\boxed{4}}$ 27. $\frac{2}{\boxed{3}} = \frac{64}{96}$

Mixed Review

Tell whether you would use a bar, line, or circle graph to display the data.

28. The number of students in each grade at your school ____bar____

29. A hospital patient's temperature taken each hour for 8 hours ____line____

30. The part of each day you spend at various activities ____circle____

Mixed Numbers and Fractions

Vocabulary

Complete.

1. A _____ mixed number _____ has a whole-number part and a fraction part.

Write the fraction as a mixed number or a whole number.

2. $\frac{20}{5}$ 3. $\frac{19}{4}$ 4. $\frac{22}{7}$ 5. $\frac{39}{10}$ 6. $\frac{19}{10}$

   _4_   _$4\frac{3}{4}$_   _$3\frac{1}{7}$_   _$3\frac{9}{10}$_   _$1\frac{9}{10}$_

7. $\frac{75}{15}$ 8. $\frac{44}{13}$ 9. $\frac{50}{7}$ 10. $\frac{63}{21}$ 11. $\frac{41}{8}$

   _5_   _$3\frac{5}{13}$_   _$7\frac{1}{7}$_   _3_   _$5\frac{1}{8}$_

12. $\frac{25}{6}$ 13. $\frac{72}{12}$ 14. $\frac{55}{9}$ 15. $\frac{46}{5}$ 16. $\frac{77}{11}$

   $4\frac{1}{6}$ _6_   _$6\frac{1}{9}$_   _$9\frac{1}{5}$_   _7_

Write the mixed number as a fraction.

17. $6\frac{2}{7}$ 18. $4\frac{6}{11}$ 19. $9\frac{2}{3}$ 20. $11\frac{1}{5}$ 21. $2\frac{2}{3}$

   $\frac{44}{7}$ _$\frac{50}{11}$_   _$\frac{29}{3}$_   _$\frac{56}{5}$_   _$\frac{8}{3}$_

22. $7\frac{2}{9}$ 23. $12\frac{4}{5}$ 24. $4\frac{5}{8}$ 25. $8\frac{2}{3}$ 26. $13\frac{1}{2}$

   $\frac{65}{9}$ _$\frac{64}{5}$_   _$\frac{37}{8}$_   _$\frac{26}{3}$_   _$\frac{27}{2}$_

Mixed Review

Write the prime factorization of each number using exponents.

27. 84   28. 72   29. 300

   $2^2 \times 3 \times 7$ $2^3 \times 3^2$ $2^2 \times 3 \times 5^2$

Write the fraction in simplest form.

30. $\frac{35}{45}$ 31. $\frac{36}{42}$ 32. $\frac{56}{72}$ 33. $\frac{22}{55}$ 34. $\frac{18}{81}$

   $\frac{7}{9}$ _$\frac{6}{7}$_   _$\frac{7}{9}$_   _$\frac{2}{5}$_   _$\frac{2}{9}$_

35. $\frac{24}{30}$ 36. $\frac{16}{40}$ 37. $\frac{24}{36}$ 38. $\frac{27}{63}$ 39. $\frac{72}{88}$

   $\frac{4}{5}$ _$\frac{2}{5}$_   _$\frac{2}{3}$_   _$\frac{3}{7}$_   _$\frac{9}{11}$_

Compare and Order

Compare. Write $<$, $>$, or $=$ for each ●.

1. $\dfrac{5}{6}$ ● $\dfrac{3}{4}$ $\underline{>}$
2. $\dfrac{1}{4}$ ● $\dfrac{1}{5}$ $\underline{>}$
3. $\dfrac{2}{3}$ ● $\dfrac{3}{8}$ $\underline{>}$
4. $\dfrac{5}{8}$ ● $\dfrac{3}{4}$ $\underline{<}$

5. $\dfrac{9}{10}$ ● $\dfrac{7}{8}$ $\underline{>}$
6. $\dfrac{7}{12}$ ● $\dfrac{3}{4}$ $\underline{<}$
7. $\dfrac{13}{16}$ ● $\dfrac{5}{6}$ $\underline{<}$
8. $\dfrac{1}{7}$ ● $\dfrac{1}{6}$ $\underline{<}$

9. $\dfrac{2}{5}$ ● $\dfrac{5}{6}$ $\underline{<}$
10. $\dfrac{9}{15}$ ● $\dfrac{3}{5}$ $\underline{=}$
11. $\dfrac{4}{7}$ ● $\dfrac{3}{5}$ $\underline{<}$
12. $\dfrac{7}{8}$ ● $\dfrac{17}{20}$ $\underline{>}$

13. $\dfrac{4}{5}$ ● $\dfrac{16}{20}$ $\underline{=}$
14. $\dfrac{7}{9}$ ● $\dfrac{2}{3}$ $\underline{>}$
15. $1\dfrac{1}{9}$ ● $1\dfrac{2}{3}$ $\underline{<}$
16. $1\dfrac{5}{9}$ ● $1\dfrac{6}{11}$ $\underline{>}$

Use the number line to order the fractions from least to greatest.

17. $\dfrac{1}{6}, \dfrac{5}{12}, \dfrac{1}{3}$

$\dfrac{1}{6}, \dfrac{1}{3}, \dfrac{5}{12}$

18. $\dfrac{5}{6}, \dfrac{7}{12}, \dfrac{1}{2}$

$\dfrac{1}{2}, \dfrac{7}{12}, \dfrac{5}{6}$

19. $\dfrac{3}{4}, \dfrac{11}{12}, \dfrac{2}{3}$

$\dfrac{2}{3}, \dfrac{3}{4}, \dfrac{11}{12}$

20. $\dfrac{2}{3}, \dfrac{7}{12}, \dfrac{5}{12}$

$\dfrac{5}{12}, \dfrac{7}{12}, \dfrac{2}{3}$

21. $\dfrac{1}{2}, \dfrac{5}{6}, \dfrac{1}{6}$

$\dfrac{1}{6}, \dfrac{1}{2}, \dfrac{5}{6}$

22. $\dfrac{7}{12}, \dfrac{1}{6}, \dfrac{1}{3}$

$\dfrac{1}{6}, \dfrac{1}{3}, \dfrac{7}{12}$

Order the fractions from least to greatest.

23. $\dfrac{1}{4}, \dfrac{1}{6}, \dfrac{2}{5}$

$\dfrac{1}{6}, \dfrac{1}{4}, \dfrac{2}{5}$

24. $\dfrac{4}{5}, \dfrac{2}{3}, \dfrac{3}{10}$

$\dfrac{3}{10}, \dfrac{2}{3}, \dfrac{4}{5}$

25. $\dfrac{1}{5}, \dfrac{3}{8}, \dfrac{4}{5}$

$\dfrac{1}{5}, \dfrac{3}{8}, \dfrac{4}{5}$

26. $\dfrac{7}{8}, \dfrac{4}{5}, \dfrac{9}{10}$

$\dfrac{4}{5}, \dfrac{7}{8}, \dfrac{9}{10}$

27. $\dfrac{3}{4}, \dfrac{7}{10}, \dfrac{5}{7}$

$\dfrac{7}{10}, \dfrac{5}{7}, \dfrac{3}{4}$

28. $1\dfrac{3}{5}, 1\dfrac{1}{8}, 1\dfrac{3}{10}$

$1\dfrac{1}{8}, 1\dfrac{3}{10}, 1\dfrac{3}{5}$

Mixed Review

Find the mean, median, and mode.

29. 6, 6, 2, 4, 8, 6, 5, 3

5, 5.5, 6

30. 23, 26, 24, 19, 31, 33

26, 25, no mode

31. 12, 9, 21, 11, 15, 15, 8

13, 12, 15

Name _____

Fractions, Decimals, and Percents

Write the decimal as a fraction.

1. 0.5 $\frac{5}{10}$ **2.** 0.14 $\frac{14}{100}$ **3.** 0.06 $\frac{6}{100}$ **4.** 0.83 $\frac{83}{100}$

5. 0.62 $\frac{62}{100}$ **6.** 0.317 $\frac{317}{1,000}$ **7.** 0.805 $\frac{805}{1,000}$ **8.** 0.955 $\frac{955}{1,000}$

Write as a decimal. Tell whether the decimal terminates or repeats.

9. $\frac{3}{10}$ 0.3, T **10.** $\frac{6}{9}$ $0.\overline{6}$, R **11.** $\frac{7}{12}$ $0.58\overline{3}$, R **12.** $\frac{11}{20}$ 0.55, T

13. $\frac{7}{30}$ $0.2\overline{3}$, R **14.** $\frac{9}{10}$ 0.9, T **15.** $\frac{7}{15}$ $0.4\overline{6}$, R **16.** $\frac{4}{11}$ $0.\overline{36}$, R

Compare. Write $<$, $>$, or $=$ for each ● .

17. 0.24 ● $\frac{1}{4}$ $<$ **18.** 0.18 ● $\frac{7}{50}$ $>$ **19.** $\frac{4}{10}$ ● 0.44 $<$

20. $\frac{1}{5}$ ● 0.19 $>$ **21.** $\frac{7}{20}$ ● 0.45 $<$ **22.** $\frac{9}{20}$ ● 0.45 $=$

Write the fraction as a percent.

23. $\frac{3}{5}$ 60% **24.** $\frac{17}{100}$ 17% **25.** $\frac{4}{2}$ 200% **26.** $\frac{1}{500}$ 0.2%

27. $\frac{9}{25}$ 36% **28.** $\frac{7}{5}$ 140% **29.** $\frac{6}{40}$ 15% **30.** $\frac{17}{20}$ 85%

Mixed Review

Estimate. Possible estimates are given.

31. $56.09 \div 7.1$ **32.** $64.1 - 13.9$ **33.** $97.6 \div 9.8$ **34.** $\$1.79 - \$0.82$

8 50 10 \$1.00

35. 188.2×21.3 **36.** $602.5 + 102.4$ **37.** $\$49.34 \times 5$ **38.** $711.2 + 798.5$

4,000 700 \$250 1,500

Evaluate the expression.

39. $6 + 4 \times 3$ 18 **40.** $18 - 6 + 2$ 14 **41.** $(10 \times 3) \div 6$ 5

© Harcourt

Practice PW41

Name _____

Estimate Sums and Differences

Use the number line to tell whether the fraction is closest to 0, $\frac{1}{2}$, or 1. Write *close to 0, close to $\frac{1}{2}$, or close to 1.*

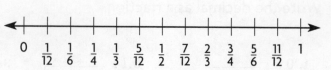

$$0 \quad \frac{1}{12} \quad \frac{1}{6} \quad \frac{1}{4} \quad \frac{1}{3} \quad \frac{5}{12} \quad \frac{1}{2} \quad \frac{7}{12} \quad \frac{2}{3} \quad \frac{3}{4} \quad \frac{5}{6} \quad \frac{11}{12} \quad 1$$

1. $\frac{2}{3}$

close to $\frac{1}{2}$
_____

2. $\frac{1}{12}$

close to 0
_____

3. $\frac{11}{12}$

close to 1
_____

4. $\frac{1}{3}$

close to $\frac{1}{2}$
_____

Estimate the sum or difference. Possible estimates are given.

5. $\frac{4}{5} + \frac{1}{8}$

1
_____

6. $\frac{5}{6} - \frac{2}{3}$

$\frac{1}{2}$
_____

7. $\frac{1}{10} + \frac{4}{7}$

$\frac{1}{2}$
_____

8. $\frac{3}{4} + \frac{9}{10}$

2
_____

9. $5\frac{3}{5} + 1\frac{7}{8}$

$7\frac{1}{2}$
_____

10. $6\frac{10}{11} - 3\frac{1}{15}$

4
_____

11. $4\frac{2}{9} + 3\frac{6}{7}$

8
_____

12. $8\frac{7}{9} - 3\frac{11}{12}$

5
_____

13. $\frac{1}{7} + \frac{9}{11}$

1
_____

14. $\frac{4}{7} - \frac{1}{2}$

0
_____

15. $\frac{5}{11} + \frac{8}{10}$

$1\frac{1}{2}$
_____

16. $\frac{3}{4} - \frac{1}{9}$

1
_____

17. $9\frac{11}{14} - 1\frac{7}{10}$

$8\frac{1}{2}$
_____

18. $5\frac{2}{3} + 4\frac{1}{6}$

$9\frac{1}{2}$
_____

19. $8\frac{5}{7} - 3\frac{4}{5}$

$4\frac{1}{2}$
_____

20. $6\frac{7}{16} - 4\frac{5}{6}$

$1\frac{1}{2}$
_____

Use a range to estimate each sum or difference. Possible estimates are given.

21. $7\frac{3}{4} - 1\frac{1}{12}$

$6\frac{1}{2}$ to 7; $6\frac{3}{4}$
_____

22. $12\frac{1}{4} - 4\frac{1}{8}$

8 to $8\frac{1}{2}$; $8\frac{1}{4}$
_____

23. $13\frac{8}{9} + 1\frac{1}{4}$

15 to $15\frac{1}{2}$; $15\frac{1}{4}$
_____

24. $6\frac{2}{15} + 4\frac{3}{4}$

$10\frac{1}{2}$ to 11; $10\frac{3}{4}$
_____

Mixed Review

Write the fraction in simplest form.

25. $\frac{15}{20}$ $\frac{3}{4}$ _____

26. $\frac{16}{28}$ $\frac{4}{7}$ _____

27. $\frac{48}{96}$ $\frac{1}{2}$ _____

28. $\frac{28}{36}$ $\frac{7}{9}$ _____

29. $\frac{5}{45}$ $\frac{1}{9}$ _____

30. $\frac{8}{32}$ $\frac{1}{4}$ _____

31. $\frac{36}{63}$ $\frac{4}{7}$ _____

32. $\frac{25}{125}$ $\frac{1}{5}$ _____

Evaluate the expression for $m = 8$ and $n = 3$.

33. $4 + m \div 2$ 8 _____

34. $6 \times n + 7$ 25 _____

35. $15 - n \times 2$ 9 _____

PW42   Practice

© Harcourt

Name _____

Add and Subtract Fractions

Use the LCD to rewrite the problem by using equivalent fractions.

1. $\frac{3}{8} + \frac{1}{2}$

$\frac{3}{8} + \frac{4}{8}$

2. $\frac{3}{4} - \frac{1}{6}$

$\frac{9}{12} - \frac{2}{12}$

3. $\frac{2}{3} + \frac{4}{5}$

$\frac{10}{15} + \frac{12}{15}$

4. $\frac{8}{9} - \frac{1}{3}$

$\frac{8}{9} - \frac{3}{9}$

5. $\frac{1}{4} + \frac{3}{7}$

$\frac{7}{28} + \frac{12}{28}$

Write the sum or difference in simplest form. Estimate to check.

6. $\frac{1}{2} + \frac{1}{5}$

$\frac{7}{10}$

7. $\frac{6}{7} - \frac{1}{4}$

$\frac{17}{28}$

8. $\frac{9}{10} - \frac{3}{5}$

$\frac{3}{10}$

9. $\frac{7}{8} - \frac{1}{2}$

$\frac{3}{8}$

10. $\frac{3}{4} + \frac{5}{8}$

$1\frac{3}{8}$

11. $\frac{4}{5} - \frac{1}{3}$

$\frac{7}{15}$

12. $\frac{5}{8} + \frac{1}{10}$

$\frac{29}{40}$

13. $\frac{1}{2} - \frac{1}{6}$

$\frac{1}{3}$

14. $\frac{7}{10} + \frac{1}{4}$

$\frac{19}{20}$

15. $\frac{5}{6} + \frac{1}{3}$

$1\frac{1}{6}$

16. $\frac{11}{12} - \frac{1}{4}$

$\frac{2}{3}$

17. $\frac{3}{10} + \frac{1}{2}$

$\frac{4}{5}$

18. $\frac{3}{4} + \frac{1}{12}$

$\frac{5}{6}$

19. $\frac{6}{7} - \frac{1}{3}$

$\frac{11}{21}$

20. $\frac{4}{5} - \frac{1}{6}$

$\frac{19}{30}$

21. $\frac{3}{4} + \frac{1}{2}$

$1\frac{1}{4}$

22. $\frac{2}{3} - \frac{3}{8}$

$\frac{7}{24}$

23. $\frac{3}{5} + \frac{1}{15}$

$\frac{2}{3}$

24. $\frac{13}{14} - \frac{2}{7}$

$\frac{9}{14}$

25. $\frac{1}{3} - \frac{1}{5}$

$\frac{2}{15}$

26. $\frac{7}{10} - \frac{2}{5}$

$\frac{3}{10}$

27. $\frac{1}{7} + \frac{1}{2}$

$\frac{9}{14}$

28. $\frac{7}{12} - \frac{1}{4}$

$\frac{1}{3}$

29. $\frac{7}{15} - \frac{2}{5}$

$\frac{1}{15}$

30. $\frac{2}{5} + \frac{1}{3}$

$\frac{11}{15}$

31. $\frac{4}{9} + \frac{1}{2}$

$\frac{17}{18}$

32. $\frac{2}{3} - \frac{2}{7}$

$\frac{8}{21}$

33. $\frac{5}{8} + \frac{1}{3}$

$\frac{23}{24}$

34. $\frac{2}{3} + \frac{1}{9}$

$\frac{7}{9}$

35. $\frac{5}{6} - \frac{1}{2}$

$\frac{1}{3}$

Mixed Review

Find the mean, median, and mode.

36. 57, 71, 50, 57, 53, 60

58, 57, 57

37. 21, 25, 29, 18, 31, 27, 24

25, 25, no mode

Find the quotient.

38. $26.98 \div 3.8$ ___7.1___

39. $1.365 \div 0.07$ ___19.5___

40. $174.08 \div 27.2$ ___6.4___

Add and Subtract Mixed Numbers

Draw a diagram to find each sum or difference. Write the answer in simplest form. Check students' diagrams.

1. $1\frac{2}{5} + 1\frac{2}{5}$ _____ $2\frac{4}{5}$

2. $2\frac{3}{8} - 1\frac{1}{4}$ _____ $1\frac{1}{8}$

3. $2\frac{1}{6} + 1\frac{1}{3}$ _____ $3\frac{3}{6}$, or $3\frac{1}{2}$

4. $3\frac{1}{2} - 1\frac{1}{4}$ _____ $2\frac{1}{4}$

5. $2\frac{3}{8} + 1\frac{1}{2}$ _____ $3\frac{7}{8}$

6. $2\frac{2}{3} - 1\frac{1}{6}$ _____ $1\frac{3}{6}$, or $1\frac{1}{2}$

Write the sum or difference in simplest form. Estimate to check.

7. $1\frac{1}{5} + 1\frac{1}{4}$ _____ $2\frac{9}{20}$

8. $2\frac{1}{2} - 1\frac{1}{8}$ _____ $1\frac{3}{8}$

9. $8\frac{5}{12} - 1\frac{1}{4}$ _____ $7\frac{1}{6}$

10. $1\frac{1}{6} + 2\frac{2}{3}$ _____ $3\frac{5}{6}$

11. $4\frac{3}{4} - 2\frac{3}{8}$ _____ $2\frac{3}{8}$

12. $2\frac{1}{2} + 4\frac{4}{5}$ _____ $7\frac{3}{10}$

13. $5\frac{7}{9} - 3\frac{2}{3}$ _____ $2\frac{1}{9}$

14. $4\frac{3}{5} - 3\frac{1}{10}$ _____ $1\frac{1}{2}$

15. $1\frac{1}{6} + 4\frac{3}{4}$ _____ $5\frac{11}{12}$

16. $7\frac{1}{3} - 2\frac{1}{4}$ _____ $5\frac{1}{12}$

17. $5\frac{5}{6} - 1\frac{2}{3}$ _____ $4\frac{1}{6}$

18. $3\frac{2}{5} + 4\frac{1}{6}$ _____ $7\frac{17}{30}$

19. $3\frac{1}{2} + 1\frac{5}{8}$ _____ $5\frac{1}{8}$

20. $3\frac{7}{8} + 4\frac{1}{3}$ _____ $8\frac{5}{24}$

21. $6\frac{5}{8} - 2\frac{2}{5}$ _____ $4\frac{9}{40}$

Mixed Review

Write the fraction as a percent.

22. $\frac{1}{4}$ _____ 25%

23. $\frac{3}{10}$ _____ 30%

24. $\frac{2}{5}$ _____ 40%

25. $\frac{5}{100}$ _____ 5%

26. $\frac{10}{5}$ _____ 200%

27. $\frac{9}{50}$ _____ 18%

Write the numbers in order from least to greatest.

28. 0.303, 0.03, 0.33, 0.033

_____ 0.03, 0.033, 0.303, 0.33 _____

29. 11.10, 10.01, 11.01, 10.10

_____ 10.01, 10.10, 11.01, 11.10 _____

30. 2.292, 2.922, 2.929, 2.229

_____ 2.229, 2.292, 2.922, 2.929 _____

31. 0.545, 0.55, 0.445, 0.45

_____ 0.445, 0.45, 0.545, 0.55 _____

32. 6.626, 6.266, 6.226, 6.662

_____ 6.226, 6.266, 6.626, 6.662 _____

33. 7.070, 70.07, 7.007, 7.707

_____ 7.007, 7.070, 7.707, 70.07 _____

Name _____

Subtract Mixed Numbers

Write the difference in simplest form. Estimate to check.

1. $8\frac{3}{4} - 6\frac{1}{2}$
$2\frac{1}{4}$

2. $4\frac{1}{5} - 2\frac{7}{10}$
$1\frac{1}{2}$

3. $7\frac{1}{4} - 2\frac{2}{3}$
$4\frac{7}{12}$

4. $5\frac{2}{9} - 3\frac{2}{3}$
$1\frac{5}{9}$

5. $3\frac{1}{5} - 2\frac{3}{10}$
$\frac{9}{10}$

6. $5\frac{3}{8} - 4\frac{1}{2}$
$\frac{7}{8}$

7. $6\frac{1}{3} - 2\frac{3}{4}$
$3\frac{7}{12}$

8. $1\frac{7}{9} - 1\frac{2}{3}$
$\frac{1}{9}$

9. $4\frac{2}{3} - 1\frac{1}{2}$
$3\frac{1}{6}$

10. $5\frac{4}{5} - 3\frac{1}{4}$
$2\frac{11}{20}$

11. $3\frac{1}{3} - 1\frac{4}{9}$
$1\frac{8}{9}$

12. $4\frac{5}{8} - 2\frac{1}{2}$
$2\frac{1}{8}$

13. $5\frac{1}{6} - 3\frac{2}{3}$
$1\frac{1}{2}$

14. $4\frac{3}{5} - 2\frac{7}{10}$
$1\frac{9}{10}$

15. $4\frac{1}{8} - 2\frac{3}{4}$
$1\frac{3}{8}$

16. $3\frac{1}{2} - 1\frac{4}{5}$
$1\frac{7}{10}$

17. $5\frac{1}{4} - 2\frac{3}{8}$
$2\frac{7}{8}$

18. $6\frac{1}{4} - 4\frac{2}{5}$
$1\frac{17}{20}$

19. $9\frac{3}{8} - 4\frac{1}{3}$
$5\frac{1}{24}$

20. $5\frac{1}{6} - 1\frac{5}{8}$
$3\frac{13}{24}$

Evaluate each expression for $a = 3\frac{1}{3}, b = 2\frac{1}{4}, c = 5\frac{1}{6}$.

21. $c - a$
$1\frac{5}{6}$

22. $c - b$
$2\frac{11}{12}$

23. $a - b$
$1\frac{1}{12}$

Mixed Review

Write in exponential form.

24. $5 \times 5 \times 5 \times 5$ ____ 5^4 ____

25. $10 \times 10 \times 10$ ____ 10^3 ____

26. $k \times k \times k \times k \times k$ ____ k^5 ____

27. $w \times w$ ____ w^2 ____

Evaluate each expression.

28. $17.61 - s$, for $s = 12.18$
5.43

29. $75.6 \div v$, for $v = 6.3$
12

30. $5f$, for $f = 8.7$
43.5

Problem Solving Strategy: Draw a Diagram

Solve by drawing a diagram.

1. In the school art room the students use square tables. Each side of a table is $4\frac{1}{2}$ ft. If some of the tables are placed end-to-end, they form a rectangle with a perimeter of 36 ft. How many tables are used to make the rectangle?

_____ 3 tables _____

2. The art room is on one side of the hallway with an office, a classroom, and the music room. The art room is between the classroom and the office. The classroom is between the music room and the art room. Which two rooms are on the ends of the hallway?

_____ office, music room _____

3. During art class, 2 students can sit on each side of a square table. The students decide to make a large rectangular table by placing 5 square tables end-to-end. How many students will be able to sit at this large table?

_____ 24 students _____

4. Richard is cutting a hole in a wall to hold an air conditioner. The front of the air conditioner is a rectangle 26 in. wide and 16 in. high. The wall is 72 in. wide. If the air conditioner is centered in the wall, how wide will the wall be on either side of it?

_____ 23 in. _____

5. Cassandra is training for a charity walk between two towns. The towns are 12 mi apart. On her first day of training, she walks $4\frac{1}{2}$ mi. If she increases her distance by $1\frac{1}{2}$ mi every 3 days, how many days will it take until Cassandra has walked at least 10 mi?

_____ 13 days _____

6. Marla wants to wrap a present that is in the shape of a cube. She wants to put one piece of ribbon around the top, bottom and two sides. She wants to put a second piece around the top, bottom, and other two sides. The box is $8\frac{1}{2}$ in. on each edge. What is the shortest length of ribbon she needs?

_____ 68 in. _____

Mixed Review

Write the number in standard form.

7. six hundred and three tenths ___600.3___

8. ninety-one hundredths ___0.91___

9. ninety and seven hundredths ___90.07___

10. eighty and nine tenths ___80.9___

Find the GCF for each set of numbers.

11. 10, 15   12. 16, 40   13. 18, 45   14. 20, 28   15. 24, 56

___5___   ___8___   ___9___   ___4___   ___8___

© Harcourt

Name _____

Estimate Products and Quotients

Estimate each product or quotient. Possible answers are given.

1. $4\frac{1}{4} \times 3\frac{3}{4}$ ___16___

2. $20\frac{5}{6} \div 6\frac{3}{4}$ ___3___

3. $\frac{3}{4} \times \frac{5}{6}$ ___1___

4. $\frac{3}{4} \div \frac{2}{3}$ ___1___

5. $45\frac{1}{3} \div 8\frac{2}{3}$ ___5___

6. $17\frac{2}{7} \times 1\frac{2}{7}$ ___17___

7. $2\frac{3}{5} \div \frac{2}{5}$ ___5___

8. $19 \times 6\frac{1}{3}$ ___114___

9. $2\frac{3}{4} \times 2\frac{4}{5}$ ___9___

10. $36\frac{3}{7} \div 11\frac{3}{4}$ ___3___

11. $\frac{7}{9} \times 13\frac{1}{9}$ ___13___

12. $\frac{1}{5} \div 20$ ___0___

13. $3\frac{3}{4} \div 4\frac{1}{2}$ ___1___

14. $42\frac{1}{6} \times 14\frac{4}{9}$ ___630___

15. $\frac{1}{10} \times \frac{1}{10}$ ___0___

16. $8\frac{1}{3} \times 6\frac{4}{5}$ ___56___

17. $12\frac{1}{6} \div 3\frac{2}{3}$ ___3___

18. $40\frac{2}{9} \div 7\frac{4}{5}$ ___5___

19. $10\frac{5}{6} \times 3\frac{7}{8}$ ___44___

20. $18\frac{3}{10} \div 1\frac{6}{7}$ ___9___

21. $9\frac{3}{4} \times 17\frac{1}{5}$ ___170___

Estimate to compare. Write $<$ or $>$ for each ●.

22. $3\frac{1}{8} \times 5$ ● $12 \div \frac{9}{10}$ ___>___

23. $6\frac{1}{2} \div 12$ ● $\frac{5}{8} \div 1\frac{2}{3}$ ___>___

24. $5\frac{2}{7} \div 1\frac{3}{8}$ ● $2\frac{1}{8} \div 3\frac{7}{8}$ ___>___

25. $3\frac{3}{4} \times 1\frac{1}{4}$ ● $31\frac{3}{4} \div 8\frac{1}{4}$ ___>___

26. $15\frac{1}{5} \div 4\frac{2}{3}$ ● $1\frac{3}{4} \div 3\frac{4}{5}$ ___>___

27. $7\frac{2}{9} \times 1\frac{3}{7}$ ● $36\frac{1}{2} \div 2\frac{7}{8}$ ___<___

Mixed Review

Write the fraction as a percent.

28. $\frac{3}{4}$ ___75%___

29. $\frac{7}{10}$ ___70%___

30. $\frac{1}{20}$ ___5%___

31. $\frac{3}{25}$ ___12%___

32. $\frac{29}{50}$ ___58%___

33. $\frac{13}{10}$ ___130%___

34. $\frac{1}{8}$ ___12.5%___

35. $\frac{5}{8}$ ___62.5%___

Multiply Fractions

Make a model to find the product. Check students' models.

1. $\frac{1}{2} \times 6$

   3

2. $\frac{2}{5} \times \frac{1}{2}$

   $\frac{1}{5}$

3. $\frac{1}{8} \times \frac{1}{2}$

   $\frac{1}{16}$

4. $10 \times \frac{1}{2}$

   5

5. $\frac{1}{2} \times \frac{1}{3}$

   $\frac{1}{6}$

Multiply. Write the answer in simplest form.

6. $\frac{1}{4} \times \frac{1}{6}$

   $\frac{1}{24}$

7. $\frac{1}{5} \times \frac{1}{2}$

   $\frac{1}{10}$

8. $\frac{3}{8} \times \frac{1}{4}$

   $\frac{3}{32}$

9. $\frac{3}{5} \times \frac{1}{4}$

   $\frac{3}{20}$

10. $\frac{4}{5} \times \frac{1}{2}$

    $\frac{2}{5}$

11. $\frac{1}{4} \times \frac{8}{9}$

    $\frac{2}{9}$

12. $\frac{3}{4} \times \frac{2}{7}$

    $\frac{3}{14}$

13. $\frac{5}{9} \times \frac{9}{10}$

    $\frac{1}{2}$

14. $\frac{5}{6} \times \frac{2}{5}$

    $\frac{1}{3}$

15. $\frac{6}{7} \times \frac{2}{3}$

    $\frac{4}{7}$

16. $\frac{3}{4} \times \frac{8}{9}$

    $\frac{2}{3}$

17. $\frac{3}{4} \times \frac{8}{15}$

    $\frac{2}{5}$

18. $\frac{1}{6} \times \frac{8}{9}$

    $\frac{4}{27}$

19. $\frac{7}{8} \times 24$

    21

20. $\frac{3}{8} \times \frac{1}{3}$

    $\frac{1}{8}$

21. $\frac{5}{6} \times \frac{3}{10}$

    $\frac{1}{4}$

22. $\frac{9}{10} \times \frac{2}{3}$

    $\frac{3}{5}$

23. $30 \times \frac{4}{5}$

    24

24. $\frac{1}{2} \times \frac{12}{13}$

    $\frac{6}{13}$

25. $\frac{9}{11} \times \frac{22}{27}$

    $\frac{2}{3}$

Compare. Write $<$, $>$, or $=$ for ●.

26. $\frac{1}{2} \times \frac{2}{3}$ ● $\frac{2}{3}$ $<$

27. $\frac{3}{4} \times 8$ ● 6 $=$

28. $\frac{1}{4} \times 4$ ● $\frac{1}{4}$ $>$

Mixed Review

Write each mixed number as a fraction.

29. $4\frac{2}{5}$

    $\frac{22}{5}$

30. $6\frac{3}{7}$

    $\frac{45}{7}$

31. $2\frac{8}{11}$

    $\frac{30}{11}$

32. $5\frac{3}{5}$

    $\frac{28}{5}$

Write each fraction as a mixed number.

33. $\frac{12}{7}$

    $1\frac{5}{7}$

34. $\frac{41}{12}$

    $3\frac{5}{12}$

35. $\frac{25}{6}$

    $4\frac{1}{6}$

36. $\frac{50}{9}$

    $5\frac{5}{9}$

© Harcourt

Name _____

Multiply Mixed Numbers

Multiply. Write your answer in simplest form.

1. $2\frac{1}{2} \times 1\frac{1}{3}$
$3\frac{1}{3}$

2. $3\frac{1}{5} \times 2\frac{1}{2}$
8

3. $8\frac{3}{4} \times \frac{2}{5}$
$3\frac{1}{2}$

4. $3\frac{1}{3} \times 1\frac{1}{5}$
4

5. $3\frac{1}{3} \times 2\frac{2}{5}$
8

6. $1\frac{3}{4} \times \frac{3}{14}$
$\frac{3}{8}$

7. $4\frac{2}{5} \times \frac{10}{11}$
4

8. $\frac{6}{7} \times 2\frac{1}{10}$
$1\frac{4}{5}$

9. $3\frac{1}{2} \times 1\frac{1}{4}$
$4\frac{3}{8}$

10. $2\frac{3}{5} \times 1\frac{2}{3}$
$4\frac{1}{3}$

11. $4\frac{3}{8} \times \frac{1}{2}$
$2\frac{3}{16}$

12. $6\frac{4}{5} \times \frac{5}{8}$
$4\frac{1}{4}$

13. $2\frac{1}{4} \times 3\frac{1}{5}$
$7\frac{1}{5}$

14. $9\frac{1}{3} \times 1\frac{2}{7}$
12

15. $\frac{3}{5} \times 1\frac{2}{3}$
1

16. $12\frac{1}{3} \times 1\frac{1}{2}$
$18\frac{1}{2}$

17. $1\frac{1}{8} \times \frac{1}{3}$
$\frac{3}{8}$

18. $3\frac{3}{4} \times 1\frac{5}{6}$
$6\frac{7}{8}$

19. $2\frac{2}{5} \times 1\frac{5}{8}$
$3\frac{9}{10}$

20. $5\frac{3}{5} \times 1\frac{2}{7}$
$7\frac{1}{5}$

Use the Distributive Property to multiply.

21. $7 \times 4\frac{1}{6}$
$29\frac{1}{6}$

22. $1\frac{1}{4} \times 8$
10

23. $5\frac{3}{8} \times 3$
$16\frac{1}{8}$

24. $6 \times 2\frac{4}{5}$
$16\frac{4}{5}$

Compare. Write $<$, $>$, or $=$ for ⬤.

25. $2\frac{1}{2} \times 2\frac{3}{4}$ ⬤ $3\frac{1}{2} \times 4$ $<$

26. $6\frac{2}{3} \times 3\frac{3}{5}$ ⬤ $3\frac{3}{4} \times 6\frac{2}{5}$ $=$

Mixed Review

Use the data in the chart for 27–28.

Quiz Scores								
30	27	21	27	25	30	29	19	15
26	27	28	22	25	23	26	18	17

27. Make a stem-and-leaf plot of the data.

28. Use the stem-and-leaf plot to find the median and mode.

25.5; 27

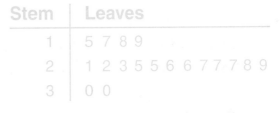

Stem	Leaves
1	5 7 8 9
2	1 2 3 5 5 6 6 7 7 7 8 9
3	0 0

Divide Fractions and Mixed Numbers

Write the reciprocal of the number.

1. $\frac{6}{7}$

2. $\frac{1}{9}$

3. 5

4. $\frac{8}{5}$

5. $3\frac{1}{3}$

$\frac{7}{6}$

9

$\frac{1}{5}$

$\frac{5}{8}$

$\frac{3}{10}$

Find the quotient. Write the answer in simplest form.

6. $\frac{4}{5} \div \frac{8}{15}$

7. $\frac{7}{10} \div \frac{1}{2}$

8. $\frac{5}{6} \div \frac{1}{2}$

9. $24 \div \frac{1}{2}$

$1\frac{1}{2}$

$1\frac{2}{5}$

$1\frac{2}{3}$

48

10. $9 \div \frac{1}{6}$

11. $\frac{7}{9} \div \frac{2}{3}$

12. $\frac{9}{10} \div \frac{2}{5}$

13. $\frac{9}{20} \div \frac{3}{4}$

54

$1\frac{1}{6}$

$2\frac{1}{4}$

$\frac{3}{5}$

14. $\frac{5}{8} \div \frac{5}{16}$

15. $\frac{5}{6} \div \frac{2}{3}$

16. $\frac{12}{21} \div \frac{4}{7}$

17. $\frac{5}{8} \div \frac{1}{4}$

2

$1\frac{1}{4}$

1

$2\frac{1}{2}$

18. $\frac{3}{4} \div \frac{2}{3}$

19. $\frac{5}{9} \div \frac{5}{6}$

20. $\frac{7}{8} \div 12$

21. $15 \div \frac{5}{9}$

$1\frac{1}{8}$

$\frac{2}{3}$

$\frac{7}{96}$

27

22. $\frac{5}{12} \div \frac{3}{4}$

23. $\frac{3}{8} \div 18$

24. $\frac{7}{10} \div 14$

25. $24 \div \frac{4}{5}$

$\frac{5}{9}$

$\frac{1}{48}$

$\frac{1}{20}$

30

Use mental math to find each quotient.

26. $10 \div \frac{1}{4}$

27. $12 \div \frac{1}{6}$

28. $3 \div \frac{1}{10}$

29. $15 \div \frac{1}{2}$

40

72

30

30

Mixed Review

Find the mean, median, and mode.

30. 8, 10, 12, 11, 8, 9, 10, 10

$9.75; 10; 10$

31. 228, 209, 195, 187, 251

$214; 209; \text{no mode}$

Compare. Write $<$, $>$, or $=$ for ⬤.

32. $\frac{4}{5}$ ⬤ $\frac{8}{9}$

33. $\frac{5}{13}$ ⬤ $\frac{4}{13}$

34. $\frac{6}{15}$ ⬤ $\frac{2}{5}$

35. $\frac{6}{7}$ ⬤ $\frac{14}{15}$

$<$

$>$

$=$

$<$

© Harcourt

Name _____

Problem Solving Skill: Choose the Operation

Solve. Name the operations used.

1. Marie practiced piano a total of $17\frac{1}{2}$ hr last week. If she practiced the same amount of time each day, how long did she practice daily?

$2\frac{1}{2}$ hr, division

2. Sylvan withdrew $\frac{2}{5}$ of the amount in his savings account, and spent $\frac{7}{10}$ of that money. What fraction of his total savings does he still have?

$\frac{18}{25}$, multiplication and subtraction

3. Ike practices guitar $2\frac{1}{2}$ hr per day, but Jenn only practices $\frac{3}{4}$ hr. How much longer does Ike practice?

$1\frac{3}{4}$ hr, subtraction

4. A painter is going to paint a wall that measures $2\frac{2}{3}$ yd by $4\frac{1}{2}$ yd. What is the area of the wall?

12 yd^2, multiplication

5. José gives each of his 15 patio plants $\frac{3}{4}$ qt of water daily in warm weather. How much water does José use on his plants on a warm day?

$11\frac{1}{4}$ qt, multiplication

6. José waters each of his 15 patio plants with $\frac{1}{2}$ qt water daily in cool weather. How much water can José expect to use on his patio plants during a cool week?

52.5 qt, multiplication

7. Marisol rode her scooter $1\frac{1}{2}$ mi to Athena's home, then $\frac{3}{4}$ mi to Ariel's home, then $1\frac{1}{4}$ mi back to her home. How far did Marisol ride?

$3\frac{1}{2}$ mi, addition

8. Bill can polish a car in $2\frac{3}{4}$ hr. Lara and Danny can do the same job working together in $1\frac{1}{2}$ hr. How much faster than Bill can Lara and Danny do the job when working together?

$1\frac{1}{4}$ hr faster, subtraction

Mixed Review

Write each fraction in simplest form.

9. $\frac{5}{10}$

$\frac{1}{2}$

10. $\frac{20}{50}$

$\frac{2}{5}$

11. $\frac{15}{25}$

$\frac{3}{5}$

12. $\frac{22}{32}$

$\frac{11}{16}$

13. $\frac{21}{24}$

$\frac{7}{8}$

© Harcourt

Name _____

Choose the Method

Solve. Choose mental math, a calculator, or paper and pencil.

1. $\frac{7}{8} \div \frac{1}{8}$

_____7_____

2. $\frac{1}{2} \times 9$

_____$4\frac{1}{2}$_____

3. $\frac{4}{5} \div \frac{1}{10}$

_____8_____

4. $5\frac{1}{3} \times 2\frac{3}{4}$

_____$14\frac{2}{3}$_____

5. $15 \div \frac{3}{10}$

_____50_____

6. $\frac{1}{6} \div \frac{7}{12}$

_____$\frac{2}{7}$_____

7. $4\frac{5}{6} \div 2\frac{1}{2}$

_____$1\frac{14}{15}$_____

8. $\frac{9}{10} \times 30$

_____27_____

9. $8\frac{4}{5} \div 1\frac{1}{3}$

_____$6\frac{3}{5}$_____

10. $\frac{7}{8} \times \frac{4}{5}$

_____$\frac{7}{10}$_____

11. $2\frac{2}{3} \times 1\frac{5}{6}$

_____$4\frac{8}{9}$_____

12. $\frac{1}{2} \div \frac{2}{5}$

_____$1\frac{1}{4}$_____

13. $1\frac{1}{2} \times 3\frac{3}{4}$

_____$5\frac{5}{8}$_____

14. $\frac{2}{3} \times 3\frac{7}{9}$

_____$2\frac{14}{27}$_____

15. $3\frac{1}{2} \div \frac{7}{12}$

_____6_____

16. About $\frac{2}{3}$ of all the students at Kenrose Middle School walk to school. There are 270 students in the school. How many of them walk to school?

_____180 students_____

17. Janeanne has 3 cups of sunflower seeds. For each batch of granola, she needs $\frac{3}{4}$ cup of sunflower seeds. How many batches of granola can she make?

_____4 batches_____

Mixed Review

Find the least common multiple for each set of numbers.

18. 4 and 6 _____12_____

19. 2 and 8 _____8_____

20. 4 and 10 _____20_____

21. 6 and 9 _____18_____

22. 2, 3, and 5 _____30_____

Write each mixed number as an improper fraction.

23. $3\frac{1}{3}$ _____$\frac{10}{3}$_____

24. $4\frac{5}{8}$ _____$\frac{37}{8}$_____

25. $1\frac{11}{12}$ _____$\frac{23}{12}$_____

26. $5\frac{2}{7}$ _____$\frac{37}{7}$_____

27. $9\frac{5}{6}$ _____$\frac{59}{6}$_____

© Harcourt

PW52 Practice

Write Expressions

Write an algebraic expression for the word expression.

1. 47 less than the product of y and 7

$7y - 47$

2. $\frac{3}{4}$ added to 8 times w

$8w + \frac{3}{4}$

3. q times 11, minus the product of 6 and t

$11q - 6t$

4. the difference between a and 4, divided by the sum of b and 9

$(a - 4) \div (b + 9)$

5. the product of m and 15 divided by the sum of n and 50

$15m \div (n + 50)$

6. k times 12 divided by the product of d and 3

$12k \div 3d$

Write a word expression for each. Possible expressions are given.

7. $15 - (r + s)$

fifteen decreased by the sum of

r and s

8. $\frac{g + 5}{t}$

the sum of g and 5, divided

by t

9. $k \times m + 1.5$

1.5 more than the product of

k and m

10. $\frac{20}{bc}$

twenty divided by the product

of b and c

11. $7.5n + xy$

the sum of 7.5 times n and x

times y

12. $de - \frac{1}{2}$

one-half less than the product

of d and e

Mixed Review

Find the quotient. Write the answer in simplest form.

13. $\frac{2}{3} \div \frac{1}{4}$

$2\frac{2}{3}$

14. $\frac{4}{5} \div \frac{2}{15}$

6

15. $9 \div \frac{3}{8}$

24

16. $\frac{3}{7} \div \frac{2}{5}$

$1\frac{1}{14}$

17. $8 \div \frac{1}{4}$

32

18. $\frac{9}{10} \div \frac{5}{6}$

$1\frac{2}{25}$

19. $12 \div \frac{4}{7}$

21

20. $\frac{14}{15} \div \frac{2}{5}$

$2\frac{1}{3}$

Evaluate Expressions

Evaluate the expression for $x = 5, 1, 2,$ and 3.

1. $4x - 2$

    18, 2, 6, 10

2. $13 - 2x$

    3, 11, 9, 7

3. $7 + 5x$

    32, 12, 17, 22

4. $\frac{3}{4} + 3x$

    $15\frac{3}{4}, 3\frac{3}{4}, 6\frac{3}{4}, 9\frac{3}{4}$

5. $(10 - 6) \cdot (x + 3)$

    32, 16, 20, 24

6. $\frac{12}{x + 1} + 8$

    10, 14, 12, 11

7. $25 - x^2$

    0, 24, 21, 16

8. $6x \div 3$

    10, 2, 4, 6

9. $4 \cdot (x + 5)$

    40, 24, 28, 32

Simplify the expression. Then evaluate the expression for the given value of the variable.

10. $4x - x + 21$ for $x = 5$

    $3x + 21$; 36

11. $7k - k + 11$ for $k = 3$

    $6k + 11$; 29

12. $6a - 3b + 27 - 2a$
    for $a = 7$ and $b = 6$

    $4a - 3b + 27$; 37

13. $m + 30 - 2n + 4m$
    for $m = 6$ and $n = 15$

    $5m - 2n + 30$; 30

Evaluate the expression for the given values of the variables.

14. $4f \cdot (h - g)$
    for $f = 2, g = 10,$ and $h = 12$

    16

15. $r \cdot (6s + 2t)$
    for $r = 4, s = 5,$ and $t = 9$

    192

Mixed Review

Compare. Write $<$ or $>$.

16. $1.50 \underline{\;<\;} 1.55$

17. $\frac{2}{3} \underline{\;>\;} \frac{1}{3}$

18. $0.80 \underline{\;>\;} \frac{3}{4}$

19. $\frac{2}{7} \underline{\;<\;} \frac{5}{6}$

Find the product.

20. 20×6

    120

21. 12×8

    96

22. 7×11

    77

23. 15×15

    225

24. 7×40

    280

25. 35×0

    0

26. 9×12

    108

27. 10×11

    110

Expressions with Squares and Square Roots

Evaluate the expression.

1. $\sqrt{16} + 9$

_____13_____

2. $34 - \sqrt{36}$

_____28_____

3. $11 + \sqrt{49} - 3$

_____15_____

4. $64 - \sqrt{64}$

_____56_____

5. $2^2 + 10 + \sqrt{25}$

_____19_____

6. $\sqrt{16} \times 3$

_____12_____

7. $\sqrt{64} \div 8 \times 1$

_____1_____

8. $9^2 \div 9 + 9$

_____18_____

9. $12^2 \div 6 \times 3$

_____72_____

10. $51 - \sqrt{64} \times 6$

_____3_____

11. $(12 + \sqrt{4}) - 14$

_____0_____

12. $5 \times (7 - 2^2)$

_____15_____

13. $\sqrt{121} + 3 \times 5^2$

_____86_____

14. $6(\sqrt{81} - \sqrt{64})$

_____6_____

15. $196 \div \sqrt{4} \times 2$

_____196_____

Evaluate the expression for the given value of the variable.

16. $x^2 + \sqrt{64}$ for $x = 6$

_____44_____

17. $\sqrt{121} - \sqrt{m} + 5$ for $m = 100$

_____6_____

18. $55 - (h + 3)$ for $h = \sqrt{49}$

_____45_____

19. $\sqrt{4} \times y^2 + 3$ for $y = 5$

_____53_____

20. $(r^2 + \sqrt{16}) \div 2$ for $r = 8$

_____34_____

21. $7a^2 - \sqrt{a}$ for $a = 4$

_____110_____

Mixed Review

Find the product. Write the answer in simplest form.

22. $\frac{3}{5} \times \frac{2}{3}$

_____$\frac{2}{5}$_____

23. $\frac{5}{8} \times \frac{2}{5}$

_____$\frac{1}{4}$_____

24. $\frac{1}{2} \times \frac{3}{4}$

_____$\frac{3}{8}$_____

25. $\frac{2}{3} \times \frac{1}{6}$

_____$\frac{1}{9}$_____

Compare. Write $<$, $>$, or $=$ in the $\bigcirc$.

26. $\frac{1}{2} \times \frac{2}{3}$ $\bigcirc<$ $\frac{2}{3}$

27. $\frac{1}{3} \times 9$ $\bigcirc<$ 5

28. $\frac{1}{7} \times 7$ $\bigcirc>$ $\frac{1}{7}$

Words and Equations

Write an equation for the word sentence. Choice of variable may vary.

1. 12 less than a number equals 15.

$$n - 12 = 15$$

2. The quotient of a number and 7 is 63.

$$n \div 7 = 63 \text{ or } \frac{n}{7} = 63$$

3. 5 more than a number is 31.

$$n + 5 = 31$$

4. 6 less than a number r is 16.

$$r - 6 = 16$$

5. 3 times the price p equals $9.45.

$$3p = \$9.45$$

6. 4 times the number of cars is 84.

$$4c = 84$$

7. A number x divided by 2.5 is 3.5.

$$x \div 2.5 = 3.5 \text{ or } \frac{x}{2.5} = 3.5$$

8. 12 fewer than a number m is $17\frac{1}{2}$.

$$m - 12 = 17\frac{1}{2}$$

9. 5 times the number of students in the class is 155.

$$5n = 155$$

10. The number of auditorium seats divided by 3 is 174.

$$x \div 3 = 174 \text{ or } \frac{x}{3} = 174$$

11. Eight more than your test score is 100.

$$t + 8 = 100$$

12. The difference between a number k and 7 is 12.

$$k - 7 = 12$$

Mixed Review

Rewrite the problem so that the divisor is a whole number.

13. $9.2 \div 5.4$

$$92 \div 54$$

14. $7.3 \div 2.6$

$$73 \div 26$$

15. $19.12 \div 3.4$

$$191.2 \div 34$$

16. $67.3 \div 0.18$

$$6,730 \div 18$$

Write the fraction in simplest form.

17. $\frac{7}{21}$

$$\frac{1}{3}$$

18. $\frac{16}{30}$

$$\frac{8}{15}$$

19. $\frac{9}{24}$

$$\frac{3}{8}$$

20. $\frac{15}{50}$

$$\frac{3}{10}$$

21. $\frac{20}{45}$

$$\frac{4}{9}$$

22. $\frac{12}{18}$

$$\frac{2}{3}$$

23. $\frac{10}{15}$

$$\frac{2}{3}$$

24. $\frac{24}{36}$

$$\frac{2}{3}$$

25. $\frac{33}{55}$

$$\frac{3}{5}$$

26. $\frac{16}{24}$

$$\frac{2}{3}$$

© Harcourt

Solve Addition Equations

Solve and check.

1. $x + 9 = 14$

_____ $x = 5$ _____

2. $m + 3.5 = 9$

_____ $m = 5.5$ _____

3. $12 + w = 23$

_____ $w = 11$ _____

4. $t + 8.7 = 16.3$

_____ $t = 7.6$ _____

5. $b + 4\frac{1}{3} = 11$

_____ $b = 6\frac{2}{3}$ _____

6. $15 = e + 11.2$

_____ $e = 3.8$ _____

7. $n + 6\frac{3}{5} = 9$

_____ $n = 2\frac{2}{5}$ _____

8. $18.9 + c = 31.2$

_____ $c = 12.3$ _____

9. $24.6 = 15.7 + h$

_____ $h = 8.9$ _____

10. $14\frac{1}{2} + d = 22$

_____ $d = 7\frac{1}{2}$ _____

11. $5\frac{1}{4} = 2\frac{1}{2} + z$

_____ $z = 2\frac{3}{4}$ _____

12. $k + 17.8 = 42.1$

_____ $k = 24.3$ _____

13. $9.3 = 5.9 + q$

_____ $q = 3.4$ _____

14. $51 = 29.8 + p$

_____ $p = 21.2$ _____

15. $j + 4 = 7$

_____ $j = 3$ _____

16. $8.6 + s = 14.3$

_____ $s = 5.7$ _____

17. $18 = y + 6$

_____ $y = 12$ _____

18. $17\frac{3}{5} = a + 8\frac{1}{2}$

_____ $a = 9\frac{1}{10}$ _____

Mixed Review

Estimate. Possible estimates are given.

19. $67.9 - 39.6$

_____ 30 _____

20. $109.4 \div 22$

_____ 5 _____

21. $\$7.78 + \$6.19$

_____ \$14 _____

22. 1.9×15.1

_____ 30 _____

23. $3 \times \$51.99$

_____ \$150 _____

24. $202.1 - 58.3$

_____ 140 _____

25. $6.71 + 19.03$

_____ 26 _____

26. $599.2 \div 3.9$

_____ 150 _____

Write the corresponding decimal or percent.

27. 16% ___0.16___

28. 7% ___0.07___

29. 0.65 ___65%___

30. 19% ___0.19___

31. 0.54 ___54%___

32. 0.02 ___2%___

33. 10% ___0.1 or 0.10___

34. 0.42 ___42%___

35. 90% ___0.90 or 0.9___

36. 0.09 ___9%___

Solve Subtraction Equations

Solve and check.

1. $t - 1 = 9$

$t = 10$

2. $12 = x - 3$

$x = 15$

3. $b - 6 = 2$

$b = 8$

4. $4 = a - 3$

$a = 7$

5. $y - 4 = 19$

$y = 23$

6. $1 = n - 50$

$n = 51$

7. $c - 1.5 = 7$

$c = 8.5$

8. $4.4 = h - 13.4$

$h = 17.8$

9. $k - 7.3 = 12.7$

$k = 20$

10. $4\frac{1}{3} = z - \frac{2}{3}$

$z = 5$

11. $f - 8\frac{3}{4} = 5$

$f = 13\frac{3}{4}$

12. $10\frac{5}{8} = w - 8$

$w = 18\frac{5}{8}$

13. $36.5 = g - 18.6$

$g = 55.1$

14. $e - 2\frac{1}{3} = 4\frac{1}{2}$

$e = 6\frac{5}{6}$

15. $42 = v - 3\frac{2}{9}$

$v = 45\frac{2}{9}$

16. $m - 31 = 2\frac{1}{4}$

$m = 33\frac{1}{4}$

17. $6.8 = p - 14.5$

$p = 21.3$

18. $s - 1.9 = 5.4$

$s = 7.3$

Mixed Review

Solve and check.

19. $22.4 = 13.5 + x$

$x = 8.9$

20. $2\frac{1}{4} + n = 6$

$n = 3\frac{3}{4}$

21. $d + 12 = 21$

$d = 9$

22. $9 = 5 + a$

$a = 4$

Find the sum or difference. Write the answer in simplest form.

23. $4\frac{2}{3} + 7\frac{3}{4}$

$12\frac{5}{12}$

24. $8\frac{5}{8} - 1\frac{2}{5}$

$7\frac{9}{40}$

25. $2\frac{5}{6} + 3\frac{1}{3}$

$6\frac{1}{6}$

26. $3\frac{1}{8} - 1\frac{3}{4}$

$1\frac{3}{8}$

27. $1\frac{3}{4} - 1\frac{1}{6}$

$\frac{7}{12}$

28. $3\frac{1}{2} + 4\frac{3}{5}$

$8\frac{1}{10}$

29. $5\frac{5}{7} - 1\frac{1}{2}$

$4\frac{3}{14}$

30. $5\frac{1}{3} - 2\frac{5}{6}$

$2\frac{1}{2}$

Problem Solving Strategy: Write an Equation

For 1 and 2, use the information below. Solve by writing an equation.

Mrs. White starts with the numbers 7 and 13. Her class adds them to get the next number, 20. Then they add 13 and 20 to get the next number, 33. The class continues to extend the number pattern.

1. In the pattern, the number 364 comes after 225. What number comes before 225?

   _____ $a + 225 = 364, a = 139$ _____

2. In the pattern, what number comes between 589 and 1,542?

   _____ $589 + b = 1,542, b = 953$ _____

For 3 and 4, use the information below.

An empty shipping box weighs 3 ounces. When filled, the box weighs 22 ounces.

3. Which equation could you use to find the weight of the contents of the shipping box?

   A $3 + w = 22$ **C** $22 + w = 3$

   B $w - 3 = 22$ **D** $w - 22 = 3$

4. How much do the contents of the shipping box weigh?

   F 3 oz   **H** 22 oz

   G 19 oz   **J** 25 oz

Solve.

5. Katrina had $89.55 when she went shopping. She bought a bedspread for $45.89 and a pair of shoes. She had $12.35 left when she got home. How much did the pair of shoes cost?

   _____ $31.31 _____

6. Leo, Pam, Dan, and Sue went bowling. Pam finished in last place. Leo scored more points than Pam, but fewer points than Dan. Sue scored fewer points than Leo. Who had the highest score?

   _____ Dan _____

Mixed Review

Determine whether the first number listed is divisible by the second number.

7. 845; 9

   _____ no _____

8. 236; 4

   _____ yes _____

9. 7,053; 3

   _____ yes _____

10. 4,312; 6

   _____ no _____

Tell whether the number is prime or composite.

11. 31

   _____ prime _____

12. 63

   _____ composite _____

13. 59

   _____ prime _____

14. 87

   _____ composite _____

Solve Multiplication and Division Equations

Solve and check.

1. $3y = 9$

$y = 3$

2. $4p = 24$

$p = 6$

3. $\frac{x}{2} = 7$

$x = 14$

4. $\frac{s}{3} = 5$

$s = 15$

5. $20 = 4n$

$n = 5$

6. $32 = 8k$

$k = 4$

7. $7 = \frac{a}{9}$

$a = 63$

8. $4 = \frac{m}{8}$

$m = 32$

9. $2x = 8$

$x = 4$

10. $3c = 18$

$c = 6$

11. $\frac{a}{4} = 8$

$a = 32$

12. $\frac{m}{5} = 4$

$m = 20$

13. $6 = \frac{k}{4}$

$k = 24$

14. $60 = 5y$

$y = 12$

15. $11 = \frac{b}{6}$

$b = 66$

16. $45 = 3n$

$n = 15$

17. $140 = 14g$

$g = 10$

18. $513 = \frac{w}{3}$

$w = 1{,}539$

19. $1{,}320 = 22d$

$d = 60$

20. $19 = \frac{g}{11}$

$g = 209$

Solve and check.

21. $\frac{12}{17} = \frac{k}{68}$

$k = 48$

22. $\frac{x}{7} = 9\frac{1}{3}$

$x = 65\frac{1}{3}$

23. $\frac{5}{8}n = 3\frac{3}{4}$

$n = 6$

24. $\frac{2}{3}m = 2\frac{1}{6}$

$m = 3\frac{1}{4}$

Mixed Review

Solve and check.

25. $a - 11 = 27$

$a = 38$

26. $18.4 = b - 3.69$

$b = 22.09$

27. $c - 6\frac{1}{3} = 14\frac{2}{3}$

$c = 21$

28. $1\frac{5}{8} + n = 5\frac{1}{4}$

$n = 3\frac{5}{8}$

Multiply. Write the answer in simplest form.

29. $2\frac{1}{4} \times 3\frac{2}{3}$

$8\frac{1}{4}$

30. $9\frac{1}{5} \times 1\frac{3}{4}$

$16\frac{1}{10}$

31. $4\frac{3}{8} \times 2\frac{2}{5}$

$10\frac{1}{2}$

32. $2\frac{2}{5} \times 1\frac{2}{3}$

4

33. $6\frac{3}{5} \times 2\frac{1}{3}$

$15\frac{2}{5}$

34. $2\frac{2}{3} \times 3\frac{3}{8}$

9

35. $1\frac{1}{2} \times 5\frac{5}{6}$

$8\frac{3}{4}$

36. $1\frac{1}{4} \times 3\frac{1}{5}$

4

Name _____

Use Formulas

Use the formula $d = rt$ to complete.

1. $d =$ _____80 mi_____
$r = 20$ mi per hr
$t = 4$ hr

2. $d =$ _____714 ft_____
$r = 17$ ft per sec
$t = 42$ sec

3. $d =$ _____51.94 km_____
$r = 9.8$ km per hr
$t = 5.3$ hr

4. $d = 75$ mi

$r =$ _____25 mi per hr_____
$t = 3$ hr

5. $d = 1,320$ km

$r =$ _____6 km per min_____
$t = 220$ min

6. $d = 99$ ft

$r =$ _____9 ft per sec_____
$t = 11$ sec

7. $d = 605$ mi
$r = 55$ mi per hr

$t =$ _____11 hr_____

8. $d = 336$ ft
$r = 28$ ft per sec

$t =$ _____12 sec_____

9. $d = 500$ ft
$r = 25$ ft per min

$t =$ _____20 min_____

Convert the temperature to degrees Fahrenheit. Write your answer as a decimal.

10. $30°C$
86°F

11. $25°C$
77°F

12. $50°C$
122°F

13. $13°C$
55.4°F

14. $3°C$
37.4°F

15. $60°C$
140°F

16. $22°C$
71.6°F

17. $54°C$
129.2°F

18. $7°C$
44.6°F

19. $100°C$
212°F

20. $15°C$
59°F

21. $0°C$
32°F

Convert the temperature to degrees Celsius. Write your answer as a decimal and round to the nearest tenth of a degree.

22. $71°F$
21.7°C

23. $50°F$
10°C

24. $140°F$
60°C

25. $90°F$
32.2°C

26. $45°F$
7.2°C

27. $121°F$
49.4°C

28. $32°F$
0°C

29. $49°F$
9.4°C

30. $96°F$
35.6°C

31. $130°F$
54.4°C

32. $113°F$
45°C

33. $86°F$
30°C

Mixed Review

Solve and check.

34. $x + 6 = 15$
$x = 9$

35. $35 = a + 16$
$a = 19$

36. $21 = 4\frac{1}{3} + m$
$m = 16\frac{2}{3}$

37. $y + 4 + 3 = 12$
$y = 5$

Estimate. Possible estimates are given.

38. 5.4×19.7
100

39. $41.6 \div 6.8$
6

40. $187.51 - 90.4$
100

41. $276.7 + 389.5$
700

© Harcourt

Problem Solving Strategy: Work Backward

Solve the problem by working backward.

1. Keesha went to the movies with her brother, Merle, and spent $15.00. The tickets cost $4.50 each. She bought a box of popcorn and 2 drinks. The drinks cost $1.50 each. How much did the popcorn cost?

_____ $3.00 _____

2. Alex brought 48 cookies to school to celebrate his birthday. He gave 9 to teachers. He then shared equally the remaining cookies with his 18 class-mates and himself. How many cook-ies remained?

_____ 1 cookie _____

3. An engineer is checking wells on a hillside. He starts at his van and walks up 100 m to Well 1. He climbs down 50 m to Well 2. Then he climbs up 200 m to Well 3, which is 220 m above Well 4. How high is each well above the engineer's van?

_____ Well 1, 100 m; Well 2, 50 m; _____

_____ Well 3, 250 m; Well 4, 30 m _____

4. Karen had a bag of oats. She used $1\frac{1}{4}$ c in a meatloaf and $3\frac{1}{4}$ c to make cookies. To make granola, Karen used twice the amount of oats she used to make cookies. If there were 4 c of oats left over, how much did Karen start with?

_____ 15 c _____

5. Maya paid $174 for a car she rented for 4 days. The rate was $36 per day. Maya also had to pay $0.20 per mi after the first 200 mi driven. How many miles did Maya drive the rented car?

_____ 350 mi _____

6. Miguel poured some punch into the pitcher. Tim added 16 oz more. Bill then added enough punch to double the amount in the pitcher. The pitcher now contains 72 oz of punch. How much did Miguel pour into the pitcher?

_____ 20 oz _____

Mixed Review

Write an algebraic expression for the word expression.

7. 4.7 more than 5 times x

_____ $5x + 4.7$ _____

8. 5 less than the quotient of t and 4.2

_____ $t \div 4.2 - 5$ _____

9. the product of p, $4n$, and m

_____ $p \times 4n \times m$ _____

Find the product.

10. 9×5 ___ 45 ___

11. 15×3 ___ 45 ___

12. 8×6 ___ 48 ___

13. 22×7 ___ 154 ___

14. 12×5 ___ 60 ___

15. 105×3 ___ 315 ___

Inequalities

Graph the inequality on the number line.

1. $x > 5$

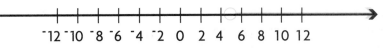

2. $x \leq {}^-2$

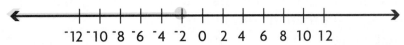

3. $x \geq {}^-1$

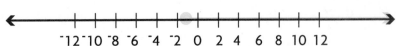

4. $x < 7$

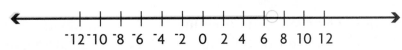

Solve and graph the inequality on the number line.

5. $x + 3 > 7$ $\underline{x > 4}$

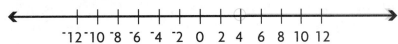

6. $n - 5 < 3$ $\underline{n < 8}$

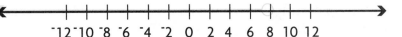

7. $2p \leq 6$ $\underline{p \leq 3}$

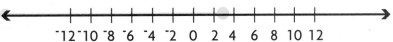

8. $k + 7 > 7$ $\underline{k > 0}$

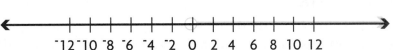

Write an inequality for the word sentence.

9. The value of m is greater than or equal to fifteen.

$$\underline{\qquad m \geq 15 \qquad}$$

10. The value of w is less than negative forty-three.

$$\underline{\qquad w < {}^-43 \qquad}$$

Mixed Review

Solve and check.

11. $\dfrac{n}{5} = 75$

$\underline{n = 375}$

12. $4a = 144$

$\underline{a = 36}$

13. $12.5 = \dfrac{d}{2.1}$

$\underline{d = 26.25}$

14. $k \div 1.05 = 8$

$\underline{k = 8.4}$

Convert to the given unit.

15. $3{,}500 \text{ lb} = \underline{1\frac{3}{4}} \text{ T}$

16. $126 \text{ in.} = \underline{3\frac{1}{2}} \text{ yd}$

17. $41 \text{ qt} = \underline{10\frac{1}{4}} \text{ gal}$

Problem Solving Strategy: Find a Pattern

Solve the problems by finding a pattern.

1. Laura read a novel she found in the school library. She read 15 pages the first day. Then each day she read 6 more pages than the day before. How many pages did she read on the eighth day?

_____ 57 pages _____

2. When Jeff played his new computer game for the first time, he scored 10,000 points. Each time he played, he increased his score by 15,000 points. How many games did Jeff have to play to reach a score of 100,000?

_____ 7 games _____

3. For her pet store's grand opening, Mrs. Santos gave 7 prizes. The seventh-prize winner received a $1 gift certificate, the sixth-prize winner a $2 certificate, the fifth-prize winner a $4 certificate, the fourth-prize winner an $8 certificate. What was the value of the first-prize certificate?

_____ $64 _____

4. Kevin is laying tile in his kitchen. The area of the kitchen is 96 ft^2. Since this is his first tile job, he is working at it slowly. He tiled 7 ft^2 the first day, 14 ft^2 the second day, and 21 ft^2 the third day. If this pattern continues, how many days will it take Kevin to tile the entire floor?

_____ 5 days _____

5. The school band is practicing for a competition to be held in 8 weeks. The band practices 1 hr a day for the first week. It practices $1\frac{1}{4}$ hr a day the second week, $1\frac{1}{2}$ hr a day the third week, and $1\frac{3}{4}$ hr a day the fourth week. If this pattern continues, how many hours a day will the band practice during the eighth week?

_____ $2\frac{3}{4}$ hr _____

6. A team of synchronized swimmers makes patterns in the water by hooking their arms and legs together. One swimmer begins the formation. After 5 sec, two swimmers join. At 10 sec, two more join. At 15 sec, another two join the group. If this pattern continues, how many swimmers will be in the group after 30 sec?

_____ 13 swimmers _____

Mixed Review

Multiply or divide. Write the answer in simplest form.

7. $\frac{1}{6} \times \frac{2}{5}$

$\frac{1}{15}$

8. $3\frac{1}{2} \times 3\frac{1}{7}$

11

9. $\frac{3}{4} \div \frac{1}{3}$

$2\frac{1}{4}$

10. $1\frac{7}{8} \div 1\frac{2}{3}$

$1\frac{1}{8}$

11. $42 + \sqrt{64} - 6^2 - \sqrt{81}$

5

12. $\sqrt{144} + 7^2 - \sqrt{36} - 5^2$

30

© Harcourt

Patterns in Sequences

Write a rule for each sequence.

1. 17, 22, 28, 35, . . .
Add increasing integers starting with 5

2. 81, 69, 57, 45, . . .
Subtract 12 from each term

3. 1, 5, 25, 125, . . .
Multiply each term by 5

4. 117, 116, 113, 108, . . .
Subtract consecutive odd integers

5. 700, 70, 7, 0.7, . . .
Divide each term by 10

6. 1,000, 500, 250, 125, . . .
Divide each term by 2

7. 77, 79, 83, 85, 89, . . .
Add 2, 4, 2, 4, 2, 4, . . .

8. 19, 16.5, 14, 11.5, . . .
Subtract 2.5 from each term

9. 64, 55, 47, 40, . . .
Subtract decreasing integers starting with 9

Find the next three possible terms in each sequence.

10. 17, 34, 68, 136, . . .
272; 544; 1,088

11. 325, 320, 310, 295, . . .
275, 250, 220

12. 14.6, 14.5, 14.3, 14.0, . . .
13.6, 13.1, 12.5

13. 3, 9, 27, 81, . . .
243, 729, 2,187

14. 535, 529, 522, 514, . . .
505, 495, 484

15. 33, 45, 57, 69, . . .
81, 93, 105

16. 1,458, 486, 162, 54, . . .
18, 6, 2

17. 390, 401, 414, 429, . . .
446, 465, 486

18. 7, 14, 28, 56, . . .
112, 224, 448

Mixed Review

Solve and check.

19. $g - 9.5 = 15.9$
$g = 25.4$

20. $47 = 26 + z$
$z = 21$

21. $16\frac{7}{12} = y + 3\frac{1}{4}$
$y = 13\frac{4}{12}$ or $13\frac{1}{3}$

Name the property shown.

22. $43 \times 1 = 43$
Identity Property of Multiplication

23. $6 + (8 + 3) = (6 + 8) + 3$
Associative Property

24. $15 \times 29 = 29 \times 15$
Commutative Property

25. $12 + 37 + 8 = 8 + 37 + 12$
Commutative Property

26. $57 + 0 = 57$
Identity Property of Addition

27. $4 \times (2 + 5) = (4 \times 2) + (4 \times 5)$
Distributive Property

Number Patterns and Functions

Write an equation to represent the function.

1.

w	3	9	15	21	33
l	1	3	5	7	11

$l = w \div 3$

2.

x	2	4	6	8	10
y	6	10	14	18	22

$y = 2x + 2$

3.

s	14	12	8	6	4
t	12.8	10.8	6.8	4.8	2.8

$t = s - 1.2$

4.

m	2	6	7	9	11
n	8	24	28	36	44

$n = 4m$

Write an equation to represent the function. Then find the missing term.

5.

j	11	15	19	23	27
k	23	27	31	35	39

$k = j + 12$

6.

a	32	26	22	18	14
b	16	13	11	9	7

$b = \frac{a}{2}$

7.

e	2	6	7	9	11
f	10	30	35	45	55

$f = 5e$

8.

x	2	3	4	5	6
y	5	8	11	14	17

$y = 3x - 1$

Write an equation for the function. Possible answers are given.

9. The width of a rectangle is $\frac{1}{3}$ its length. $w = \frac{1}{3}l$

10. An elevator travels at the rate of 5 floors per minute. $r = 5m$

11. Each person on the bus has two suitcases. $p = 2s$

Mixed Review

Write as a percent.

12. 0.002   **13.** $\frac{7}{20}$ **14.** 1.18   **15.** $\frac{1}{25}$

0.2%   35%   118%   4%

Write the prime factorization in exponent form.

16. 90   **17.** 252   **18.** 675   **19.** 500

$2 \times 3^2 \times 5$ $2^2 \times 3^2 \times 7$ $3^3 \times 5^2$ $2^2 \times 5^3$

Name _____

Geometric Patterns

Draw the next three figures in the pattern.

1.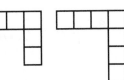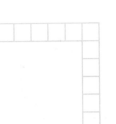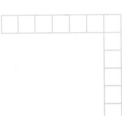

2.

3.

4.

Draw the next two figures in the pattern.

5.

6.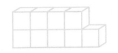

Mixed Review

Find the next three possible terms in each sequence.

7. 7, 9.6, 12.2, 14.8 . . .   **8.** 336, 329, 322, 315 . . .   **9.** 12, 36, 108, 324 . . .

_17.4, 20, 22.6_   _308, 301, 294_   _972; 2,916; 8,748_

Write the fraction as a mixed number or a whole number.

10. $\frac{51}{8}$ ___ $6\frac{3}{8}$ **11.** $\frac{19}{5}$ ___ $3\frac{4}{5}$ **12.** $\frac{23}{2}$ ___ $11\frac{1}{2}$ **13.** $\frac{91}{7}$ ___ 13

© Harcourt

Practice   PW 67

Points, Lines, and Planes

Name the geometric figure.

1.

   line segment XY

2.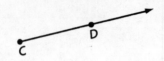

   ray CD

3.

   point A

4.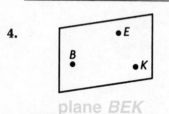

   plane BEK

5.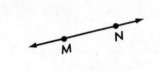

   line MN

6.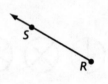

   ray RS

For Exercises 7–9, use the figure at the right.

7. Name three points.

   point A, point B, point C

8. Name four different rays.

   $\overrightarrow{AB}$ or $\overrightarrow{AC}$, $\overrightarrow{CB}$ or $\overrightarrow{CA}$, $\overrightarrow{BC}$, $\overrightarrow{BA}$

9. Name three different line segments.

   $\overline{AB}$ or $\overline{BA}$, $\overline{AC}$ or $\overline{CA}$, $\overline{BC}$ or $\overline{CB}$

Mixed Review

Solve and check.

10. $\frac{n}{5} = 40$

    $n = 200$

11. $7x = 63$

    $x = 9$

12. $25 = \frac{k}{6}$

    $k = 150$

13. $4.7 = \frac{d}{2.1}$

    $d = 9.87$

14. $84 = 7c$

    $c = 12$

15. $s \div 1.05 = 800$

    $s = 840$

16. $3m = 450$

    $m = 150$

17. $129.5 = 7g$

    $g = 18.5$

Write the sum or difference. Write the answer in simplest form.

18. $\frac{2}{3} + \frac{1}{4}$

    $\frac{11}{12}$

19. $\frac{3}{5} - \frac{1}{2}$

    $\frac{1}{10}$

20. $\frac{1}{8} + \frac{1}{6}$

    $\frac{7}{24}$

21. $\frac{5}{8} - \frac{2}{5}$

    $\frac{9}{40}$

22. $\frac{1}{3} - \frac{2}{9}$

    $\frac{1}{9}$

23. $\frac{1}{4} + \frac{3}{5}$

    $\frac{17}{20}$

24. $\frac{3}{4} - \frac{1}{3}$

    $\frac{5}{12}$

25. $\frac{3}{7} + \frac{1}{2}$

    $\frac{13}{14}$

PW68 Practice

Angle Relationships

For 1–4, use the figure at the right.

1. Name two angles adjacent to ∠AFB.

   _____∠AFE; ∠BFC_____

2. Name an angle vertical to ∠EFD.

   _____∠AFB_____

3. Name an angle that is complementary to ∠DFC.

   _____∠DFE_____

4. Name two angles that are supplementary to ∠AFE.

   _____∠AFB; ∠EFD_____

Find the unknown angle measure.

5.
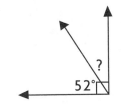

_____38°_____

6.
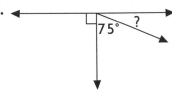

_____15°_____

7.
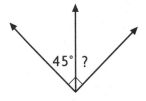

_____45°_____

8.
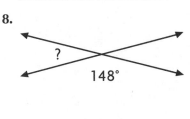

_____32°_____

9.
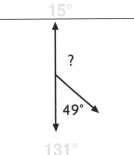

_____131°_____

10.
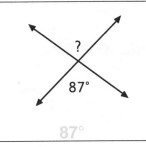

_____87°_____

Mixed Review

Solve and check.

11. $y + 9 = 14$

    _____$y = 5$_____

12. $5 + c = 17$

    _____$c = 12$_____

13. $4.3 = x + 1.8$

    _____$x = 2.5$_____

14. $p + 9\frac{1}{3} = 14\frac{2}{3}$

    _____$p = 5\frac{1}{3}$_____

Write the prime factorization in exponent form.

15. 24

    _____$2^3 \times 3$_____

16. 144

    _____$2^4 \times 3^2$_____

17. 360

    _____$2^3 \times 3^2 \times 5$_____

Lines and Angles

Classify the lines as parallel, perpendicular, or intersecting. Use the symbol ∥ or ⊥ when appropriate.

1.

intersecting

2.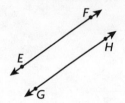

$\overleftrightarrow{EF} \parallel \overleftrightarrow{GH}$

3.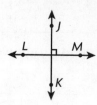

$\overleftrightarrow{LM} \perp \overleftrightarrow{JK}$

For Exercises 4–8, use the figure at the right. Possible answers are given.

4. Name all the pairs of parallel lines.

$\overleftrightarrow{CD}$ and $\overleftrightarrow{EF}$

5. Name a transversal.

$\overleftrightarrow{AB}$

6. Name all the pairs of alternate interior angles.

∠6 and ∠3; ∠7 and ∠2

7. Name all the pairs of alternate exterior angles.

∠1 and ∠8; ∠4 and ∠5

8. Name all the pairs of corresponding angles.

∠5 and ∠7; ∠6 and ∠8; ∠1 and ∠3; ∠2 and ∠4

Mixed Review

Find the sum or difference.

9. $1\frac{2}{5} + 2\frac{3}{10}$

$3\frac{7}{10}$

10. $4\frac{3}{8} - 2\frac{1}{4}$

$2\frac{1}{8}$

11. $8\frac{7}{10} - \frac{4}{5}$

$7\frac{9}{10}$

12. $\frac{11}{12} + 1\frac{2}{3}$

$2\frac{7}{12}$

13. $12.29 - 1.07$ _____ 11.22

14. $8.791 + 0.45$ _____ 9.241

15. $0.602 - 0.060$ _____ 0.542

16. $527.4 + 43.685$ _____ 571.085

17. $7.023 + 16.71$ _____ 23.733

18. $0.834 - 0.097$ _____ 0.737

© Harcourt

Polygons

Use the figure at the right.

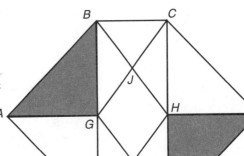

1. Name two triangles.

   _____ Possible answers: *ABG, BCJ* _____

2. Name three quadrilaterals.

   _____ Possible answers: *ABCG, GFHJ, GJHK* _____

3. Identify the polygon named *ABCHF*.

   _____ pentagon _____

4. Identify the polygon named *BCDEFA*.

   _____ hexagon _____

5. Identify the polygon named *DEFKGJBC*.

   _____ octagon _____

6. Identify the polygon named *AFEKHJG*.

   _____ 7-gon _____

7. Identify the polygon named *CGED*.

   _____ quadrilateral _____

Mixed Review

Multiply.

8. $\frac{4}{5} \times \frac{3}{4}$

   _____ $\frac{3}{5}$ _____

9. $\frac{7}{8} \times \frac{2}{3}$

   _____ $\frac{7}{12}$ _____

10. $\frac{9}{10} \times \frac{5}{6}$

    _____ $\frac{3}{4}$ _____

11. $24 \times \frac{3}{8}$

    _____ 9 _____

12. $1\frac{1}{2} \times \frac{4}{5}$

    _____ $1\frac{1}{5}$ _____

13. $\frac{3}{7} \times 2\frac{5}{8}$

    _____ $1\frac{1}{8}$ _____

14. $3\frac{1}{3} \times 2\frac{5}{6}$

    _____ $9\frac{4}{9}$ _____

15. $4\frac{3}{4} \times 1\frac{1}{5}$

    _____ $5\frac{7}{10}$ _____

Triangles

Find the measure of the missing angle and classify the triangle containing the missing angle by its angles.

1.
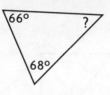
_____46°; acute_____

2.
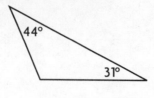
_____105°; obtuse_____

3.
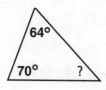
_____46°; acute_____

4.
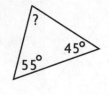
_____80°; acute_____

5.
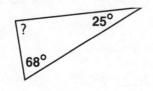
_____87°; acute_____

6.

_____70°; right_____

7.
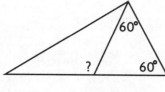
_____120°; obtuse_____

8.
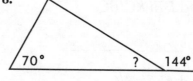
_____36°; acute_____

9.
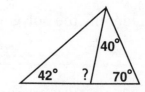
_____110°; obtuse_____

Classify each triangle by the lengths of its sides.

10.
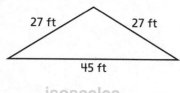
_____isosceles_____

11.
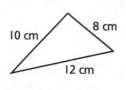
_____scalene_____

12.
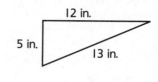
_____scalene_____

Mixed Review

Solve.

13. $24 + b = 105$

_____$b = 81$_____

14. $g - 47 = 18$

_____$g = 65$_____

15. $m + 59 = 91$

_____$m = 32$_____

Evaluate the expression.

16. $5(\sqrt{64} - 3)$ _____25_____

17. $3^2 + \sqrt{81}$ _____18_____

18. $\sqrt{100} \div 5 \times 2^2$ _____8_____

© Harcourt

PW72 **Practice**

Problem Solving Strategy: Find a Pattern

Solve the problem by finding a pattern.

1. The Auto Stop is advertising a special sale: buy 3 cans of motor oil, get 1 can free. How many cans should you buy in order to get 36 cans of motor oil?

_____ 27 cans _____

2. The Auto Stop charges $2.09 for a can of motor oil. Adam spends $37.62 on oil during the "buy 3 cans, get 1 free" sale. How many cans of oil did he get in all?

_____ 24 cans _____

3. The school cafeteria serves both ice cream and apples for dessert. Twenty-five students choose ice cream for every 6 students who choose apples. In one week, the cafeteria served 600 ice creams. How many students chose apples?

_____ 144 students _____

4. Barry and Cecilia are playing a number game. One of them thinks of a number pattern and gives the first six numbers. The other has to name the next number in the pattern. Barry gave Cecilia these numbers: 3, 4, 7, 11, 18, 29. Cecilia correctly gave the next number. What number did she give?

_____ 47 _____

5. Twenty-four students went on the school trip to the science museum. The admission price was $4.00 per student, but 1 student was admitted free for every 3 students who paid. What was the total cost?

_____ $72.00 _____

6. The floor of a 17 ft by 13 ft sun room is tiled with tiles that are 1 ft^2. The tiles alternate between black and white. If there is a black tile in one corner of the room, how many black tiles will be needed in all?

_____ 111 black tiles _____

Mixed Review

Use a property to simplify the expression. Then evaluate the expression and identify the property you used.

7. $3 + 16 + 27$

_____ 46; commutative _____

8. $(24 + 37) + 63$

_____ 124; associative _____

9. $73 + 120 + 27$

_____ 220; commutative _____

Write the fraction in simplest form.

10. $\frac{14}{48}$

$\frac{7}{24}$

11. $\frac{27}{45}$

$\frac{3}{5}$

12. $\frac{24}{60}$

$\frac{2}{5}$

13. $\frac{15}{90}$

$\frac{1}{6}$

14. $\frac{20}{64}$

$\frac{5}{16}$

Quadrilaterals

Give the most exact name for the figure.

1.

_____rhombus_____

2.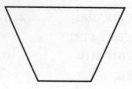

_____trapezoid_____

3.

_____quadrilateral_____

4.

_____square_____

5.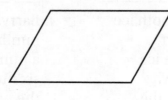

_____parallelogram_____

6.

_____rectangle_____

Complete the statement, giving the most exact name for the figure.

7. A quadrilateral with exactly one pair of parallel sides is a

_____trapezoid_____

8. A polygon with four sides and no pair of parallel sides is a

_____quadrilateral_____

Diagonals of a quadrilateral are lines drawn from one vertex to the opposite vertex. Complete the statements about diagonals.

9. If a quadrilateral has four congruent sides, but its diagonals are not congruent, then the quadrilateral is a

_____rhombus_____

10. If a quadrilateral has four congruent sides and its diagonals are congruent, then the quadrilateral is a

_____square_____

Mixed Review

Evaluate each expression.

11. $3.81 \div m$ for $m = 3$

_____1.27_____

12. $9w$ for $w = 4.7$

_____42.3_____

13. $8.02 - r$ for $r = 5.6$

_____2.42_____

Tell whether you would survey the population or use a sample. Explain.

14. You want to know how far each student in your class lives from school.

_____population; small group_____

15. You want to know the percentage of a certain model of car that is red.

_____sample; large group_____

© Harcourt

PW74   Practice

Draw Plane Figures

Draw the figure. Use square dot paper or isometric dot paper. Check students' drawings.

1. an obtuse isosceles triangle

2. a quadrilateral with opposite sides congruent and no right angles

3. a quadrilateral with exactly one pair of parallel sides

4. a pentagon with three congruent sides

5. a quadrilateral with no congruent sides

6. a triangle with all sides congruent

7. a pentagon with all sides congruent

8. a quadrilateral with four right angles and two pairs of congruent sides

9. a quadrilateral with all sides congruent and four right angles

10. a hexagon with all sides congruent

11. a rectangle with all sides congruent

12. a right scalene triangle

Mixed Review

Solve and check.

13. $8.7 = 5.8 + w$

$w = 2.9$

14. $y + 3.6 = 17.1$

$y = 13.5$

15. $23.5 + c = 35.3$

$c = 11.8$

Compare the fractions. Write $<$, $>$, or $=$ for each.

16. $\frac{1}{3}$ —$<$— $\frac{5}{9}$

17. $\frac{2}{5}$ —$>$— $\frac{3}{10}$

18. $\frac{5}{8}$ —$<$— $\frac{3}{4}$

19. $\frac{6}{10}$ —$=$— $\frac{3}{5}$

Name _____

Circles

For 1–4, use the circle at the right. Name the given parts of the circle.

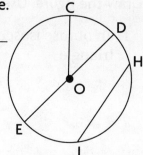

1. center _____ *O* _____   **2.** diameters _____ *DE* _____

3. radii _____ *OC, OD, OE* _____   **4.** chords other than diameters

_____ *HJ* _____

Draw and label the figure. Check students' drawings.

5. a circle with chord *ST*   **6.** a circle with center *N*   **7.** a circle with diameter *RW* and radius *XZ*

For 8–11, complete the sentence by using *must, can,* or *cannot*.

8. Two radii of the same circle _____ must _____ be equal in length.

9. Two chords of the same circle _____ can _____ be equal in length.

10. A chord drawn through the center of a circle _____ must _____ be the longest line segment that can be drawn in the circle.

11. As the size of a circle increases, the relationship between the radius and the diameter _____ cannot _____ change.

Mixed Review

Evaluate the expression.

12. $2 + 6^2 - 3 + 9$ _____ 44 _____   **13.** $9 \div 3 \times 4 + (10 - 6)$ _____ 16 _____

14. $2^3 + 4 \times 5 - 1$ _____ 27 _____   **15.** $(8 \times 6) - (4 \times 3)$ _____ 36 _____

Find the measure of each angle.

16. The complement of the angle is 18°.

_____ 72° _____

17. The supplement of the angle is 73°.

_____ 107° _____

18. The supplement of the angle is 126°.

_____ 54° _____

© Harcourt

PW76   Practice

Name _____

Congruent Segments and Angles

Use a compass to decide which two line segments in each
group are congruent.

1.
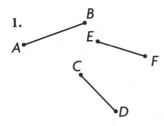

2.
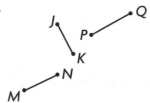

3.
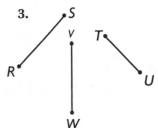

_____ $\overline{CD} \cong \overline{EF}$ _____   _____ $\overline{JK} \cong \overline{MN}$ _____   _____ $\overline{RS} \cong \overline{VW}$ _____

Find the measure of each angle, using a protractor. Then tell whether
the angles in each pair are congruent. Write *yes* or *no*.

4.
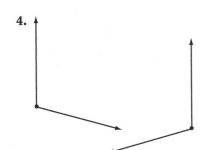

5.

6.
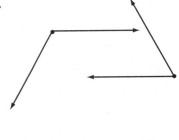

_____ 105°; yes _____   _____ 22°; yes _____   _____ 120°, 60°; no _____

7. In the space at the right, use a compass,
and a straightedge to construct a line
segment and an angle congruent to
the ones below. Check students' drawings.

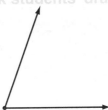

Mixed Review

Write as a decimal.

8. $\frac{3}{5}$ _____ 0.6 _____

9. $\frac{7}{10}$ _____ 0.7 _____

10. $\frac{1}{4}$ _____ 0.25 _____

11. $\frac{5}{2}$ _____ 2.5 _____

Solve.

12. $4x = 60$

13. $\frac{c}{3} = 25$

14. $36 = 9k$

15. $3.2 = \frac{s}{7}$

_____ $x = 15$ _____   _____ $c = 75$ _____   _____ $k = 4$ _____   _____ $s = 22.4$ _____

Bisect Line Segments and Angles

If a line segment of the given length is bisected, how long will each of the smaller segments be?

1. 21 in.   **2.** 1.08 m   **3.** 63.35 cm   **4.** 0.5 in.   **5.** 13 cm

___10.5 in.___   ___0.54 m___   ___31.675 cm___   ___0.25 in.___   ___6.5 cm___

If an angle of the given measure is bisected, how many degrees will there be in each of the smaller angles that are formed?

6. 84°   **7.** 27.4°   **8.** 108.5°   **9.** 12.5°   **10.** 27°

___42°___   ___13.7°___   ___54.25°___   ___6.25°___   ___13.5°___

Bisect the figures.

11.

A   B

Check students' drawings.

12.

J   K

Check students' drawings.

13.

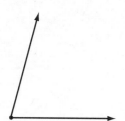

Check students' drawings.

14.

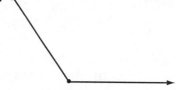

Check students' drawings.

Mixed Review

Solve.

15. $n - 12 = 23$ **16.** $g + 13.8 = 23$ **17.** $a - 64 = 15$ **18.** $2.5 + m = 7$

___$n = 35$___   ___$g = 9.2$___   ___$a = 79$___   ___$m = 4.5$___

Solve.

19. $\frac{2}{3} \times \frac{5}{8}$ **20.** $\frac{6}{7} \div \frac{1}{3}$ **21.** $\frac{4}{5} \times \frac{1}{3}$ **22.** $\frac{4}{9} \div \frac{2}{3}$

___$\frac{5}{12}$___   ___$2\frac{4}{7}$___   ___$\frac{4}{15}$___   ___$\frac{2}{3}$___

Similar and Congruent Figures

Use ~ or ≅ to compare the figures if they appear to be similar or congruent. Write *neither* if the figures appear not to be similar or congruent.

1.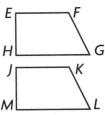

    EFGH ~ JKLM

    EFGH ≅ JKLM

2.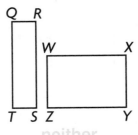

    neither

3.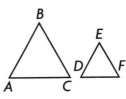

    △ABC ~ △DEF

4.

    circle X ~ circle Y

    circle X ≅ circle Y

5.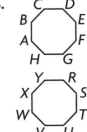

    ABCDEFGH ~ RSTUVWXY

    ABCDEFGH ≅ RSTUVWXY

6.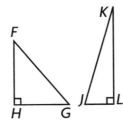

    neither

7.

    ABCD ~ EFGH

8.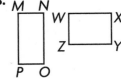

    neither

Write *true* or *false* for each statement.

9. If two figures are the same shape and size, then they must be congruent.

    true

10. If two figures are similar, then they must be congruent.

    false

Mixed Review

Solve and check.

11. $96 = 12m$ ___*m = 8*___ 12. $11p = 77$ ___*p = 7*___ 13. $95 = 5s$ ___*s = 19*___ 14. $14x = 70$ ___*x = 5*___

Evaluate each expression for $a = 3$ and $b = 5$.

15. $a^2 + b^2 - a + (7 - b)$

    33

16. $8b - 23 + (ab - 11) - 7a$

    0

Transformations of Plane Figures

Tell which type or types of transformation the second figure is of the
first figure. Write *translation*, *rotation*, or *reflection*.

1.

_____rotation_____

2.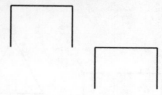

_____translation_____

3.

_____reflection_____

Draw a 90° rotation and a horizontal reflection of each original figure.
Check students' work.

4.

5.

Mixed Review

Write the decimal or percent.

6. 0.65

_____65%_____

7. 32%

_____0.32_____

8. 0.15

_____15%_____

Use the order of operations to solve.

9. $6 + 5^2 - (6 \times 4)$

_____7_____

10. $(27 \div 3) + 3^2 - 4$

_____14_____

11. $3 + (64 \div 8)$

_____11_____

PW80   Practice

Name _____

Tessellations

Make the tessellation shape described by each pattern. Then form
two rows of a tessellation by using transformations. Check students' tessellations.

1.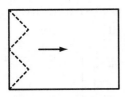

2.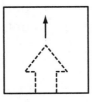

3.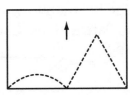

4.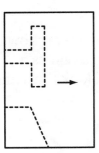

5.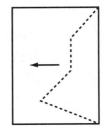

6.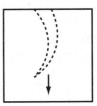

Tell whether the shape can be used to form a tessellation. Write *yes* or *no*.

7.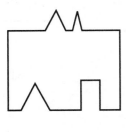

no

8.

yes

9.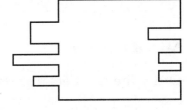

no

Mixed Review

Solve.

10. $x - 6 = 19$

25

11. $13 + x = 31$

18

12. $17 - x = 12$

5

Write the difference in simplest form.

13. $7\frac{1}{3} - 3\frac{3}{4}$

$3\frac{7}{12}$

14. $4\frac{2}{5} - 1\frac{2}{3}$

$2\frac{11}{15}$

15. $9\frac{3}{8} - \frac{4}{5}$

$8\frac{23}{40}$

16. $30 - 27\frac{7}{8}$

$2\frac{1}{8}$

© Harcourt

Name _____

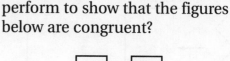

Problem Solving Strategy: Make a Model

Solve the problem by making a model.

1. Carol is making a design from the shape below. She wants the shape to tessellate a plane. Can she use this shape?

_____ yes _____

2. What transformation can you perform to show that the figures below are congruent?

_____ reflection _____

3. Are the polygons shown below congruent? Explain.

No. They have the same shape,

but they are not the same size.

4. Which of the capital letters shown below can be reflected across a vertical line and still look the same?

_____ W, X, and Y _____

Mixed Review

Order the numbers from least to greatest.

5. $0.35, \frac{1}{3}, 0.03$

$0.03, \frac{1}{3}, 0.35$

6. $\frac{3}{4}, 0.075, 0.6$

$0.075, 0.6, \frac{3}{4}$

7. $\frac{2}{3}, \frac{5}{6}, 0.7$

$\frac{2}{3}, 0.7, \frac{5}{6}$

Find the angle measures.

8. $\angle 1 =$ __95°__

9. $\angle 2 =$ __52°__

10. $\angle 3 =$ __33°__

11. $\angle 4 =$ __52°__

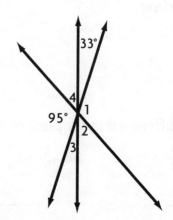

© Harcourt

PW82 Practice

Symmetry

Tell if the figure has line symmetry. If so, draw the lines of symmetry.

1.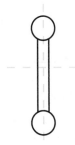

_____yes_____

2.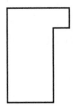

_____no_____

3.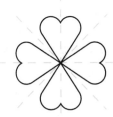

_____yes_____

Complete the other half of the figure across the line of symmetry.

4.

5.

6.

Tell whether each figure has rotational symmetry, and, if so, identify the symmetry as a fraction of a turn and in degrees.

7.

Yes; $\frac{1}{4}$; 90°

8.

Yes; $\frac{1}{2}$; 180°

9.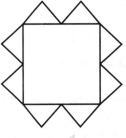

Yes; $\frac{1}{4}$; 90°

Mixed Review

Write the percent as a decimal.

10. 26%

_____0.26_____

11. 9%

_____0.09_____

12. 71%

_____0.71_____

13. 16.5%

_____0.165_____

Write the mixed number as a fraction.

14. $3\frac{3}{4}$

$\frac{15}{4}$

15. $7\frac{1}{8}$

$\frac{57}{8}$

16. $1\frac{5}{6}$

$\frac{11}{6}$

17. $10\frac{3}{5}$

$\frac{53}{5}$

Name _____

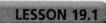

Customary Measurements

Convert to the given unit.

1. 80 fl oz = __10__ c

2. 18 pt = __9__ qt

3. 510 ft = __170__ yd

4. 720 in. = __20__ yd

5. 5 months ≈ __20__ weeks

6. 6 c = __48__ fl oz

7. 3 gal = __12__ qt

8. 6 T = __12,000__ lb

9. 32 fl oz = __4__ c

10. 5 mi = __26,400__ ft

11. 44 qt = __11__ gal

12. 10 pt = __20__ c

13. 157 ft = __52__ yd __1__ ft

14. 220 in. = __18__ ft __4__ in.

15. $5\frac{2}{3}$ yd = __17__ ft

16. $5\frac{1}{2}$ T = __11,000__ lb

17. $6\frac{1}{4}$ ft = __75__ in.

18. $7\frac{1}{2}$ ft = __$2\frac{1}{2}$__ yd

19. 325 ft = __108__ yd __1__ ft

20. $3\frac{3}{4}$ yd = __$11\frac{1}{4}$__ ft

21. 15 gal = __60__ qt

Compare. Write <, >, or = for each ⬤.

22. 8,500 lb ⬤ 4 T

___>___

23. 25 yd ⬤ 75 ft

___=___

24. 9 days ⬤ 225 hrs

___<___

25. 16 c ⬤ 4 qt

___=___

26. 5 gal ⬤ 30 pt

___>___

27. 12 ft ⬤ 120 in.

___>___

Mixed Review

Solve and check.

28. 6x = 84 __x = 14__

29. $\frac{w}{11}$ = 6 __w = 66__

30. 3.5 m = 14 __m = 4__

31. $\frac{c}{8}$ = 4.7 __c = 37.6__

32. 6.3 = $\frac{h}{20}$ __h = 126__

33. 9.9 = 1.8 r __r = 5.5__

Classify each angle as *acute, obtuse, right,* or *straight*.

34.
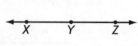
___straight___

35.
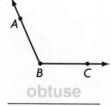
___obtuse___

36.
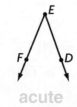
___acute___

37.
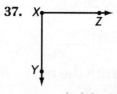
___right___

© Harcourt

Metric Measurements

Complete the pattern.

1. 1 L = __100__ cL

0.1 L = __10__ cL

0.01 L = __1__ cL

2. 1,000 mg = __1__ g

100 mg = __0.1__ g

10 mg = __0.01__ g

1 mg = __0.001__ g

3. 1 m = __0.001__ km

10 m = __0.01__ km

100 m = __0.1__ km

1,000 m = __1__ km

Convert to the given unit.

4. 40 g = __0.04__ kg

5. 300 km = __300,000__ m

6. 9 kL = __9,000__ L

7. 6 kL = __60,000__ dL

8. 300 cm = __30__ dm

9. 50 dL = __500__ cL

10. 12 kL = __12,000__ L

11. 28 g = __28,000__ mg

12. 8 km = __8,000__ m

13. 2.2 g = __220__ cg

14. 7 dm = __0.7__ m

15. 5.5 cg = __0.55__ dg

Compare. Write $<$, $>$, or = for ⬤.

16. 600 mm ⬤ 6 m

___<___

17. 80 km ⬤ 80,000 m

___=___

18. 4,000 mL ⬤ 4 L

___=___

19. 2.5 kg ⬤ 25,000 mg

___>___

20. 50 kL ⬤ 50,000 L

___=___

21. 14,500 mg ⬤ 145 g

___<___

Mixed Review

Write as a percent.

22. $\frac{3}{5}$

60%

23. $\frac{2}{8}$

25%

24. $\frac{4}{5}$

80%

25. $\frac{2}{10}$

20%

Write the difference in simplest form.

26. $7\frac{1}{2} - 6\frac{1}{3}$

$1\frac{1}{6}$

27. $5\frac{5}{8} - 3\frac{3}{4}$

$1\frac{7}{8}$

28. $10\frac{1}{6} - 5\frac{7}{8}$

$4\frac{7}{24}$

29. $15\frac{1}{3} - 12\frac{4}{5}$

$2\frac{8}{15}$

Relate Customary and Metric

Estimate the conversion. Possible answers are given.

1. 4 ft ≈ __?__ cm

_____120_____

2. 300 g ≈ __?__ oz

_____10_____

3. 12 qt ≈ __?__ L

_____12_____

4. 30 lb ≈ __?__ kg

_____14_____

5. 16 L ≈ __?__ qt

_____16_____

6. 64 cm ≈ __?__ ft

_____2_____

7. 8.5 fl oz ≈ __?__ mL

_____255_____

8. 75 mi ≈ __?__ km

_____120_____

9. 20 cm ≈ __?__ in.

_____8_____

10. 4 m ≈ __?__ in.

_____156_____

11. 150 kg ≈ __?__ lb

_____330_____

12. 375 mL ≈ __?__ fl oz

_____12.5_____

13. 2 ft ≈ __?__ cm

_____60_____

14. 80 km ≈ __?__ mi

_____50_____

15. 6 oz ≈ __?__ g

_____180_____

Compare. Write < or > for each ⬤.

16. 7 ft ⬤ 421 cm

_____<_____

17. 80 cm ⬤ 4.5 ft

_____<_____

18. 8.5 lb ⬤ 5 kg

_____<_____

19. 1 m ⬤ 5 in.

_____>_____

20. 1,000 in. ⬤ 9 m

_____>_____

21. 5 km ⬤ 7.4 mi

_____<_____

22. 3.5 oz ⬤ 150 g

_____<_____

23. 8.2 qt ⬤ 10.1 L

_____<_____

24. 1.5 mi ⬤ 1.7 km

_____>_____

Mixed Review

Solve and check.

25. $x + 7 = 19$

_____$x = 12$_____

26. $y - 9 = 7$

_____$y = 16$_____

27. $m + 19 = 41$

_____$m = 22$_____

28. $r - 27 = 15$

_____$r = 42$_____

29. $z + 4.7 = 11$

_____$z = 6.3$_____

30. $w - 7.8 = 5.6$

_____$w = 13.4$_____

Simplify.

31. $\dfrac{20}{160}$ ____$\frac{1}{8}$____

32. $\dfrac{48}{9}$ ____$5\frac{1}{3}$____

33. $\dfrac{77}{210}$ ____$\frac{11}{30}$____

34. $\dfrac{115}{15}$ ____$7\frac{2}{3}$____

Appropriate Tools and Units

Measure the line segment to the given length.

1. nearest inch; nearest half inch

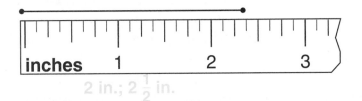

2 in.; 2 $\frac{1}{2}$ in.

2. nearest centimeter;
nearest millimeter

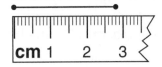

3 cm; 28 mm

3. nearest half inch; nearest quarter inch

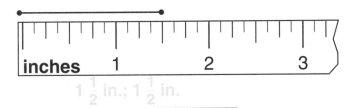

1 $\frac{1}{2}$ in.; 1 $\frac{1}{2}$ in.

4. nearest centimeter;
nearest millimeter

5 cm; 53 mm

5. nearest inch; nearest half inch

2 in.; 2 in.

6. nearest centimeter;
nearest millimeter

2 cm; 19 mm

Tell which measurement is more precise.

7. 9 lb or 142 oz

142 oz

8. 6 c or 50 fl oz

50 fl oz

9. 40 cm or 420 mm

420 mm

10. 9 mg or 1 cg

9 mg

11. 2 yd or 71 in.

71 in.

12. 1 L or 980 mL

980 mL

Name an appropriate customary or metric unit of measure for each item.

13. the amount of formula in a baby's bottle

fluid ounces or milliliters

14. the weight of a laptop computer

pounds or kilograms

15. the length of the eraser on a pencil

millimeters or parts of an inch

16. the weight of a box of tissues

ounces or grams

Mixed Review

Solve and check.

17. $5w = 30$

$w = 6$

18. $\frac{m}{4} = 5$

$m = 20$

19. $72 = 9h$

$h = 8$

20. $\frac{w}{3} = 17$

$w = 51$

Convert to the given unit.

21. $10\frac{1}{2}$ feet = _____ yds

$3\frac{1}{2}$

22. 13 gal = _____ qt

52

© Harcourt

Problem Solving Skill: Estimate or Find Exact Answer

Decide whether you need an estimate or an exact answer. Solve.

1. You and several friends are setting up tents on a camping trip. It takes 25 min to set up a tent. If you begin at 1:00 P.M., can you set up 7 tents by 3:00 P.M.?

_____ estimate; no _____

2. Your campsite is a rectangle 61 ft by 33 ft. You have 200 ft of rope. Do you have enough to run the rope around the entire perimeter of the campsite?

_____ estimate; yes _____

3. You brought 9 bags of snacks with you for the 2-day trip. Each bag cost $1.59. If you paid for the snacks with a $20 bill, how much change did you receive?

_____ exact; $5.69 _____

4. On the second day of the trip, your group hikes for $3\frac{3}{4}$ hr. If you average 3.8 mi per hr, will you have reached your goal of 10 mi for the day?

_____ estimate; yes _____

5. The odometer on the van you rented for the trip read 5,398.2 mi when you left home. It read 5,702.1 mi when you arrived back home. How far did you drive?

_____ exact; 303.9 mi _____

6. Everyone agrees that they want to get at least 8 hr sleep per night. If you want to wake up at 6:45 A.M. each morning, what is the latest you can fall asleep each night?

_____ exact; 10:45 P.M. _____

7. The trip to the campground usually takes about $3\frac{1}{4}$ hr. If you leave home at 8:45 A.M. and make two 20-min stops, would you arrive by noon?

_____ estimate; no _____

8. On the last night of the camping trip, you have 1 gal of water left. After making 3 cans of soup that each required 16 fl oz of water, how many fluid ounces of water do you have left?

_____ exact; 80 fl oz _____

Mixed Review

Write the sum or difference in simplest form.

9. $\frac{1}{2} - \frac{1}{3}$

$\frac{1}{6}$
_____

10. $\frac{2}{5} - \frac{1}{4}$

$\frac{3}{20}$
_____

11. $\frac{2}{5} - \frac{1}{6}$

$\frac{7}{30}$
_____

12. $\frac{5}{8} - \frac{1}{4}$

$\frac{3}{8}$
_____

13. $\frac{7}{8} - \frac{3}{4}$

$\frac{1}{8}$
_____

14. $\frac{7}{10} + \frac{1}{5}$

$\frac{9}{10}$
_____

15. $\frac{1}{6} + \frac{1}{3}$

$\frac{1}{2}$
_____

16. $\frac{3}{5} + \frac{1}{3}$

$\frac{14}{15}$
_____

17. $\frac{1}{9} + \frac{1}{2}$

$\frac{11}{18}$
_____

18. $\frac{2}{9} + \frac{1}{3}$

$\frac{5}{9}$
_____

Find the sum.

19. $0.314 + 7.213$

7.527
_____

20. $3.64 + 4.732$

8.372
_____

21. $0.84 + 0.217$

1.057
_____

22. $2.5 + 0.9$

3.4
_____

© Harcourt

Perimeter

Find the perimeter.

1.

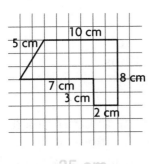

_____35 cm_____

2.

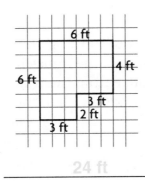

_____24 ft_____

3.

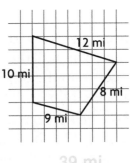

_____39 mi_____

Find the unknown length.
Then find the perimeter.

4.

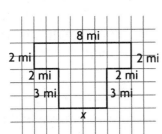

_____x = 4 mi;_____

_____26 mi_____

The perimeter is given.
Find the unknown length.

5.

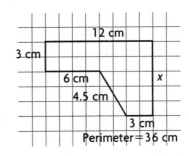

_____x = 7.5 cm_____

Mixed Review

Convert to the given unit.

6. 18 yd = __648__ in.

7. 22 qt = __$5\frac{1}{2}$__ gal

8 435 min = __$7\frac{1}{4}$__ hr

9. 8.5 gal = __68__ pt

10. 348 in. = __29__ ft

11. $12\frac{1}{2}$ lb = __200__ oz

Write a numerical or algebraic expression for the word expression.

12. One hundred divided by the sum of k and m. ___$100 \div (k + m)$, or $\frac{100}{k + m}$___

13. v less than two thousand forty-seven. ___$2{,}047 - v$___

14. w multiplied by the product of a and b. ___$w \times a \times b$, or $w(ab)$___

Problem Solving Strategy: Draw a Diagram

Solve the problem by drawing a diagram.

A contractor built a house in the shape of a rectangle. The house is 64 ft long and 48 ft wide. There is a wall running across the width of the house. The wall divides the length of the house into two sections, one larger than the other. The distance from the wall to one end of the house is 3 times the distance from the wall to the other end.

1. Describe the shape of the larger section of the house. Give the dimensions of the figure.

   ____square; each side is 48 ft____

2. Molding is going to be installed around the entire floor of the larger section of the house. How many feet of molding will be needed?

   ____192 ft____

3. There are 3 doors leading into the house. Each door is 3 ft wide. What is the perimeter of the house if the doors are not included?

   ____215 ft____

4. There are beams around the perimeter of the house every 16 in. If there is a beam in each corner, what is the total number of beams?

   ____168 beams____

5. There are plans to add a garage to the side of the house. The length of the rectangular garage will be 3 ft greater than its width. If the perimeter of the garage will be 90 ft, find its length and width.

   ____24 ft; 21 ft____

6. The short side of the garage will be attached to a short side of the house. What will be the perimeter of the house and garage when the garage is complete?

   ____272 ft____

Mixed Review

Write a rule for each sequence. Then find the sixth term.

7. 56, 48, 40, 32, . . .

   ____Subtract 8; 16.____

8. 486, 162, 54, 18, . . .

   ____Divide by 3; 2.____

9. $2, 2\frac{3}{4}, 3\frac{1}{2}, 4\frac{1}{4}, \ldots$

   ____Add $\frac{3}{4}$; $5\frac{3}{4}$.____

10. 0.07, 0.7, 7, 70, . . .

   ____Multiply by 10; 7,000.____

11. 4.6, 7.3, 10, 12.7, . . .

   ____Add 2.7; 18.1.____

12. 16, 8, 4, 2, . . .

   ____Divide by 2; $\frac{1}{2}$.____

Convert to the given unit.

13. 2,400 mL = ____2.4____ L

14. 5.8 kg = ____5,800____ g

15. 150 cm = ____1.5____ m

16. 0.7 g = ____700____ mg

17. 1,300 m = ____1.3____ km

18. 7,500 L = ____7.5____ kL

Circumference

Find the circumference of the circle. Use 3.14 or $\frac{22}{7}$ for π. Round to the nearest whole number.

1.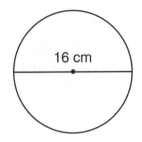

16 cm

50 cm

2.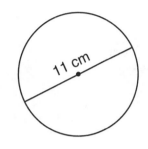

11 cm

35 cm

3.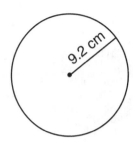

9.2 cm

58 cm

4.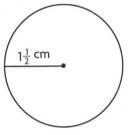

$1\frac{1}{2}$ cm

9 cm

5.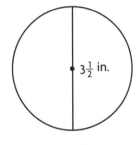

$3\frac{1}{2}$ in.

11 in.

6.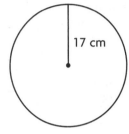

17 cm

107 cm

7.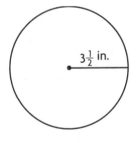

$3\frac{1}{2}$ in.

22 in.

8.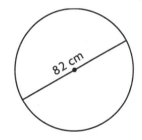

82 cm

257 cm; or 258 cm

9.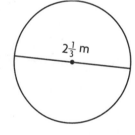

$2\frac{1}{3}$ m

7 m

Mixed Review

Solve and check.

10. $3x = 12$

   $x = 4$

11. $40 = 8m$

   $m = 5$

12. $\frac{y}{3} = 6$

   $y = 18$

13. $\frac{h}{7} = 6$

   $h = 42$

Find the perimeter.

14.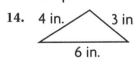

4 in.   3 in.

6 in.

13 in.

15.

9.2 cm

18 cm   7.9 cm

14 cm   11.3 cm

60.4 cm

16.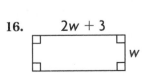

2w + 3

w

6w + 6

17.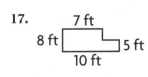

7 ft

8 ft   5 ft

10 ft

36 ft

Practice   PW91

Name _____

Estimate and Find Area

Estimate the area of the figure. Each small square on the grid represents $1\ \text{in.}^2$
Possible estimates are given.

1.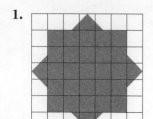
about 29 in.²

2.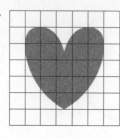
about 19 in.²

3.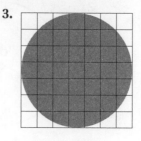
about 38 in.²

4.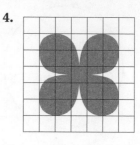
about 20 in.²

Find the area.

5.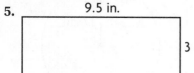
9.5 in.
3 in.
_____28.5 in.²_____

6.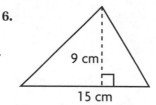
9 cm
15 cm
_____67.5 cm²_____

7.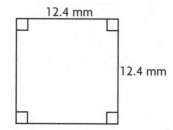
12.4 mm
12.4 mm
_____153.76 mm²_____

8.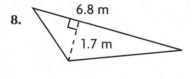
6.8 m
1.7 m
_____5.78 m²_____

9.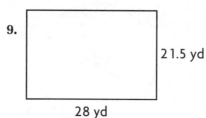
21.5 yd
28 yd
_____602 yd²_____

10.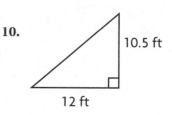
10.5 ft
12 ft
_____63 ft²_____

Mixed Review

Find the circumference of the circle. Use 3.14 for π.

11. $d = 17$ cm

12. $d = 3.5$ in.

13. $r = 11$ mm

14. $r = 6.1$ ft

_____53.38 cm_____

_____10.99 in._____

_____69.08 mm_____

_____38.308 ft_____

Solve and check.

15. $x + 7 = 19$

16. $30 = a + 13$

17. $45 = 22.5 + n$

18. $c + 2.3 = 9.1$

_____$x = 12$_____

_____$a = 17$_____

_____$n = 22.5$_____

_____$c = 6.8$_____

© Harcourt

Algebra: Areas of Parallelograms and Trapezoids

Find the area of each figure.

1.

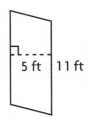

5 ft | 11 ft

_____
55 ft²

2.

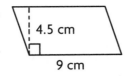

4.5 cm

9 cm

_____
40.5 cm²

3.

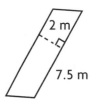

2 m

7.5 m

_____
15 m²

4.

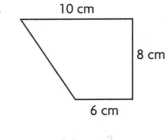

10 cm

8 cm

6 cm

_____
64 cm²

5.

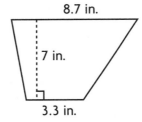

8.7 in.

7 in.

3.3 in.

_____
42 in.²

6.

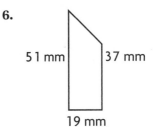

51 mm | 37 mm

19 mm

_____
836 mm²

7.

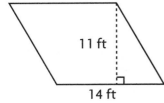

11 ft

14 ft

_____
154 ft²

8.

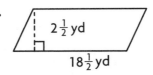

2½ yd

18½ yd

_____
46.25 yd²

9.

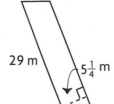

29 m

5¼ m

_____
152.25 m²

Mixed Review

Tell which measurement is more precise.

10. 1 ft or 10 in.   **11.** 2 T or 2,010 lb   **12.** 3 qt or 1 gal   **13.** 2 kg or 2,020 g

_____10 in._____   _____2,010 lb_____   _____3 qt_____   _____2,020 g_____

Evaluate the expression for $x = 0$, 2, and 4.

14. $6 - \dfrac{x}{2}$ **15.** $5x + 12$ **16.** $3x + 2$ **17.** $(x + 2) \cdot 3$

_____6, 5, 4_____   _____12, 22, 32_____   _____2, 8, 14_____   _____6, 12, 18_____

Name _____

Algebra: Areas of Circles

Find the area of each circle to the nearest whole number.
All areas are approximations.

1.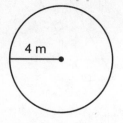
   4 m

   _____ 50 m² _____

2.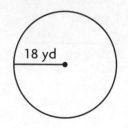
   18 yd

   _____ 1,017 yd² _____

3.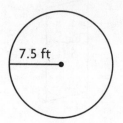
   7.5 ft

   _____ 177 ft² _____

4. $r = 17$ yd ___907 yd²___   5. $d = 38$ ft ___1,134 ft²___   6. $r = 5.6$ m ___98 m²___

7. $d = 10$ mm ___79 mm²___   8. $r = 2.2$ mi ___15 mi²___   9. $d = 54$ cm ___2,289 cm²___

10. $r = 21$ ft ___1,385 ft²___   11. $d = 1.8$ mi ___3 mi²___   12. $r = 15.5$ in. ___754 in.²___

13. $d = 30$ cm ___707 cm²___   14. $r = 6.6$ yd ___137 yd²___   15. $d = 16$ m ___201 m²___

Find the area of the partial circle to the nearest whole number. All areas are approximations.

16.
   22 mm

   _____ 190 mm² _____

17.
   6.5 yd

   _____ 33 yd² _____

Mixed Review

Convert to the given unit.

18. 32 g = ___ mg   19. 42 ft = ___ yd   20. 36 oz = ___ lb   21. 12 days = ___ hr

   ___32,000___   ___14___ $2\frac{1}{4}$ ___288___

Compare the numbers. Write $<$, $>$, or $=$ for each ◯.

22. 0.01 0.11 23. 19.9 19.90 24. 0.411 0.401 25. 1.575 ◯ 1.757

© Harcourt

Name _____

Algebra: Changing Dimensions

Find the new area when the given dimensions are doubled.

1.

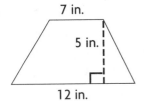
7 in.
5 in.
12 in.

_____190 in.²_____

2.

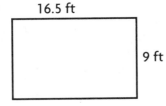
16.5 ft
9 ft

_____594 ft²_____

3.

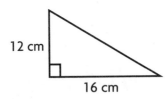
12 cm
16 cm

_____384 cm²_____

4.

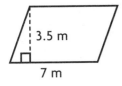
3.5 m
7 m

_____98 m²_____

5.

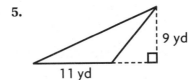
9 yd
11 yd

_____198 yd²_____

6.

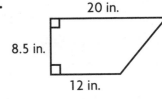
20 in.
8.5 in.
12 in.

_____544 in.²_____

7. The dimensions of an 8-in. square are halved. How do the perimeter and area of the new square compare with the perimeter and area of the original square?

The perimeter of the new square is $\frac{1}{2}$ the perimeter of the original

square. The area of the new square is $\frac{1}{4}$ the area of the original square.

8. The radius of a circle is 6 in. If the radius is doubled, how does the area of the new circle compare with the area of the original?

The area of the new circle is 4 times the area of the original circle.

Mixed Review

Complete.

9. 36 in. = ___3___ ft

10. 12 ft = ___4___ yd

11. 4 yd = ___144___ in.

12. 3 m = ___300___ cm

13. 5 km = ___5,000___ m

14. 60 mm = ___6___ cm

© Harcourt

Types of Solid Figures

Name the figure. Is it a polyhedron?

1.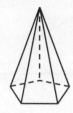

2.

3.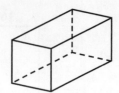

4.

1. ___pentagonal___

   ___pyramid; yes___

2. ___cone; no___

3. ___rectangular___

   ___prism; yes___

4. ___cylinder; no___

Write *true* or *false* for each statement. Rewrite each false statement as a true statement.

5. A cylinder has one base.

   ___False; a cylinder has two bases.___

6. A cone has one flat surface.

   ___True___

7. A cube has eight faces

   ___False; a cube has six faces.___

8. A square pyramid is a polyhedron.

   ___True___

9. A triangular prism has two congruent bases.

   ___True___

10. The faces of a square pyramid are squares.

    ___False; other than the base,___
    ___the faces are triangles.___

Mixed Review

Solve and check.

11. $a - 40 = 21$

    ___$a = 61$___

12. $b - 3 = 18$

    ___$b = 21$___

13. $75 = c - 48$

    ___$c = 123$___

14. $36 = d - 9$

    ___$d = 45$___

15. $14\frac{1}{2} = e - 11\frac{1}{2}$

    ___$e = 26$___

16. $7.3 = f - 4$

    ___$f = 11.3$___

Write the equal factors. Then find the value.

17. 7^3

    ___$7 \times 7 \times 7$; 343___

18. 9^2

    ___9×9; 81___

19. 4^4

    ___$4 \times 4 \times 4 \times 4$; 256___

© Harcourt

PW96 Practice

Views of Solid Figures

| Triangular Pyramid | Triangular Prism | Rectangular Pyramid | Rectangular Prism | Pentagonal Pyramid | Hexagonal Prism | Cylinder | Cone |

Name each solid figure that has the given top view. Refer to the solid figures in the box above.

1.   2.   3.   4.   5.

1. hexagonal prism
2. cone
3. rectangular prism
4. pentagonal pyramid
5. triangular prism

Name the solid figure that has the given views.

6.   7.   8.

6. cylinder   7. rectangular pyramid   8. triangular prism

Mixed Review

9. $\sqrt{100} \times (4 - 3^2) + 9^2$

31

10. $(8 - 3)^2 - (\sqrt{49} + \sqrt{4})$

16

Write each rational number in the form $\frac{a}{b}$. Possible answers are given.

11. 4.75   12. $6\frac{1}{8}$ 13. 6.3   14. $10\frac{1}{2}$

$\frac{475}{100}$ $\frac{49}{8}$ $\frac{63}{10}$ $\frac{21}{2}$

Problem Solving Strategy: Solve a Simpler Problem

Solve the problem by first *solving a simpler problem.*

1. Jon is building models of edible prisms. He uses gumdrops for vertices and licorice for edges. How many gumdrops and pieces of licorice will he need to make a prism whose base has 8 sides?

_____ 16 gumdrops and _____

_____ 24 pieces of licorice _____

2. Carol wants to make a model of a prism whose base has 9 sides. She will use balls of clay for the vertices and straws for the edges. How many balls of clay and straws will she need? How many faces will her prism have?

_____ 18 balls of clay and 27 straws; _____

_____ 11 faces _____

3. Chloe used 30 toothpicks as edges to make a model for a prism. How many sides does one base have? How many vertices does the prism have?

_____ 10 sides; 20 vertices _____

4. Dan used 12 balls of clay as vertices to make a model for a prism. How many sides does one base have? How many edges does the prism have?

_____ 6 sides; 18 edges _____

5. Marty built a model of a solid figure. It has 6 vertices and 9 edges. It has 5 faces. What is this figure?

_____ triangular prism _____

6. Nancy built a model of a solid figure. It has 5 vertices and 8 edges. It has 5 faces. What is this figure?

_____ square pyramid _____

Mixed Review

For 7–11, use the figure at the right. Find the measure of each angle.

7. ∠BCO _____ 67° _____

8. ∠BOC _____ 70° _____

9. ∠COD _____ 110° _____

10. ∠BOE _____ 110° _____

11. ∠ODC _____ 42° _____

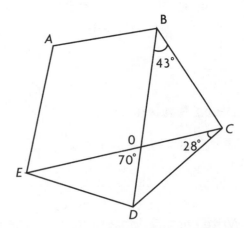

Find the sum or difference.

12. 306 + 1,229 + 558 + 74 _____ 2,167 _____

13. 45,923 + 7,192 + 19,537 _____ 72,652 _____

14. 727,401 − 204,854 _____ 522,547 _____

15. 93,144 − 3,019 _____ 90,125 _____

© Harcourt

Name _____

Algebra: Surface Area

Find the surface area. Use 3.14 for π.

1.
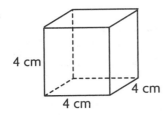
4 cm
4 cm
4 cm

_____96 cm²_____

2.
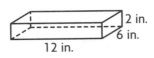
2 in.
6 in.
12 in.

_____216 in.²_____

3.
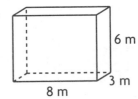
6 m
3 m
8 m

_____180 m²_____

4.
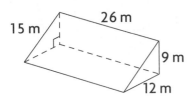
26 m
15 m
9 m
12 m

_____1,044 m²_____

5.
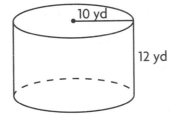
10 yd
12 yd

_____1,381.6 yd²_____

6.
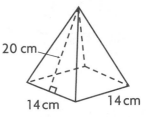
20 cm
14 cm
14 cm

_____756 cm²_____

7.
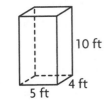
10 ft
4 ft
5 ft

_____220 ft²_____

8.
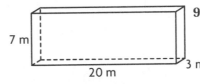
7 m
3 m
20 m

_____442 m²_____

9.
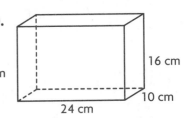
16 cm
10 cm
24 cm

_____1,568 cm²_____

Mixed Review

Evaluate the expression for $m = 6$ and $n = 2$.

10. $m \div 3 - n$

_____0_____

11. $(50 - m^2) \times 3 + n$

_____44_____

12. $30n - 5 \times m$

_____30_____

Find the LCM of each pair of numbers.

13. 4, 18 _____36_____

14. 6, 32 _____96_____

15. 3, 11 _____33_____

Name _____

Estimate and Find Volume

Find the volume.

1.
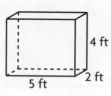
4 ft
5 ft
2 ft

40 ft³

2.
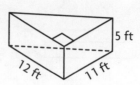
5 ft
12 ft
11 ft

330 ft³

3.
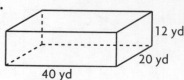
12 yd
20 yd
40 yd

9,600 yd³

4.
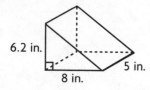
6.2 in.
5 in.
8 in.

_124 in.³_

5.
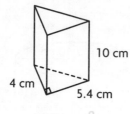
10 cm
4 cm
5.4 cm

108 cm³

6.
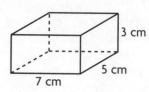
3 cm
5 cm
7 cm

105 cm³

Find the unknown length.

7.
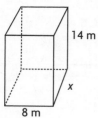
14 m
x
8 m

$V = 672$ m³

_x = 6 m_

8.
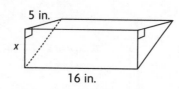
5 in.
x
16 in.

$V = 160$ in.³

_x = 4 in._

9.
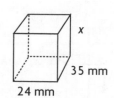
x
35 mm
24 mm

$V = 17,640$ mm³

_x = 21 mm_

Mixed Review

Find the circumference of the circle to the nearest whole number.
Use 3.14 or $\frac{22}{7}$ for π.

10. $r = 4$ in.

about 25 in.

11. $d = 6.3$ cm

about 20 cm

12. $r = 12\frac{1}{2}$ m

about 79 m

13. $d = 9\frac{1}{3}$ yd

about 29 yd

14. $r = 110$ mm

about 691 mm

15. $d = 15.7$ ft

about 49 ft

$\angle A$ measures 38°. Find each measure.

16. the measure of the
supplement of $\angle A$

measure: ___142°___

17. the measure of the
complement of $\angle A$

measure: ___52°___

PW100 Practice

© Harcourt

Problem Solving Strategy: Make a Model

Find the volume. Then double the dimensions. Find the new volume.

1.
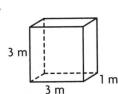
3 m
3 m
1 m

2.
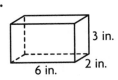
3 in.
2 in.
6 in.

3.
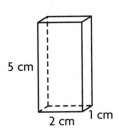
5 cm
2 cm   1 cm

4.
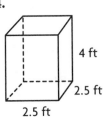
4 ft
2.5 ft
2.5 ft

___9 m³; 72 m³___   ___36 in.³; 288 in.³___   ___10 cm³; 80 cm³___   ___25 ft³; 200 ft³___

Find the volume of each prism. Then halve the underlined dimension and find the new volume.

	Length	Width	Height	Volume	New Volume
5.	5 m	4 m	2 m	40 m³	20 m³
6.	12 ft	8 ft	10 ft	960 ft³	480 ft³
7.	24 cm	3 cm	6 cm	432 cm³	216 cm³
8.	9 in.	6 in.	10 in.	540 in.³	270 in.³

Mixed Review

The area of a rectangle is 40 cm². Find the width.

9. length: 16 cm _2.5 cm_   10. length: 25 cm _1.6 cm_   11. length: 12.5 cm _3.2 cm_

Solve and check.

12. $n + 8 = 57$
$n = 49$

13. $134 = x + 82$
$x = 52$

14. $k + 2\frac{1}{3} = 11$
$k = 8\frac{2}{3}$

15. $22 = 7.34 + b$
$b = 14.66$

16. $17\frac{1}{2} + m = 23\frac{1}{4}$
$m = 5\frac{3}{4}$

17. $44 = 37 + a$
$a = 7$

Algebra: Volumes of Pyramids

Find the volume.

1.

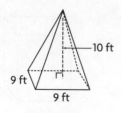

10 ft
9 ft
9 ft

_____270 ft³_____

2.

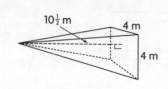

$10\frac{1}{2}$ m   4 m
4 m

_____56 m³_____

3.

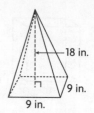

18 in.
9 in.
9 in.

_____486 in.³_____

4.

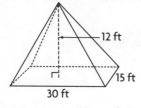

12 ft
15 ft
30 ft

_____1,800 ft³_____

5.

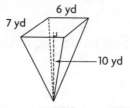

6 yd
7 yd
10 yd

_____140 yd³_____

6.

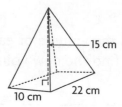

15 cm
10 cm   22 cm

_____1,100 cm³_____

7. rectangular pyramid: $l = 36$ in.,
$w = 50$ in., $h = 60$ in.

_____36,000 in.³_____

8. square pyramid: $l = 14$ yd,
$w = 14$ yd, $h = 25$ yd

_____$1,633\frac{1}{3}$ yd³_____

9. rectangular pyramid: $l = 6$ cm,
$w = 5$ cm, $h = 6$ cm

_____60 cm³_____

10. square pyramid: $l = 10$ m,
$w = 10$ m, $h = 15$ m

_____500 m³_____

Mixed Review

Find the area of each circle to the nearest whole number. Use 3.14
for π.

11. $r = 4$ yd

_____about 50 yd²_____

12. $d = 12$ ft

_____about 113 ft²_____

13. $r = 5.5$ m

_____about 95 m²_____

14. $d = 7.2$ cm

_____about 41 cm²_____

Convert to the given unit.

15. 4 qt = ___16___ c

16. 26 in. = ___$2\frac{1}{6}$___ ft

17. 68 oz = ___$4\frac{1}{4}$___ lb

18. 7 T = ___14,000___ lb

19. 4 days = ___96___ hr

20. 56 c = ___14___ qt

Name _____

Algebra: Volumes of Cylinders

Find the volume. Round to the nearest whole number.

1.

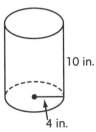

10 in.

4 in.

about 502 in.^{3}

2.

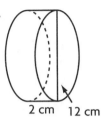

2 cm   12 cm

about 226 cm^3

3.

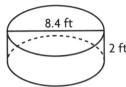

8.4 ft

2 ft

about 111 ft^3

4.

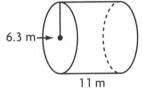

6.3 m

11 m

about 1,371 m^3

5. 1 cm

4.6 cm

about 66 cm^3

6.

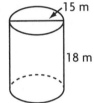

15 m

18 m

about 3,179 m^3

Find the volume of the inside cylinder to the nearest whole number.

7.

3.5 in.

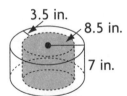

8.5 in.

7 in.

_550 in.^{3}_

8.

3.4 m

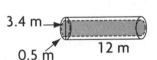

0.5 m   12 m

_54 m^3_

9.

6 ft

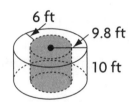

9.8 ft

10 ft

_453 ft^3_

Mixed Review

Use the formula $d = rt$ to complete.

10. $d = 200$ mi

   $r = 50$ mi per hr

   $t =$ __4__ hr

11. $d =$ __108__ ft

   $r = 12$ ft per sec

   $t = 9$ sec

12. $d = 800$ km

   $r =$ __80__ km per hr

   $t = 10$ hr

13. $d =$ __50__ cm

   $r = 250$ cm per min

   $t = 0.2$ min

14. $d = 1,980$ mi

   $r =$ __440__ mi per day

   $t = 4\frac{1}{2}$ days

15. $d = 255$ m

   $r = 20.4$ m per sec

   $t =$ __12.5__ sec

Name _____

Ratios and Rates

Write two equivalent ratios. Possible answers are given.

1. $\frac{4}{6}$

$\frac{2}{3}, \frac{8}{12}$

2. $\frac{12}{28}$

$\frac{6}{14}, \frac{3}{7}$

3. $\frac{5}{20}$

$\frac{1}{4}, \frac{10}{40}$

4. $\frac{2}{18}$

$\frac{1}{9}, \frac{3}{27}$

5. $\frac{7}{49}$

$\frac{1}{7}, \frac{3}{21}$

6. $\frac{2}{5}$

$\frac{4}{10}, \frac{8}{20}$

Write each ratio in fraction form. Then find the unit rate.

7. 7 apples for $1.00

$\frac{7 \text{ apples}}{\$1.00}$; $0.14 per apple

8. $0.72 for 12 pages

$\frac{\$0.72}{12 \text{ pages}}$; $0.06 per page

9. 24 people in 6 cars

$\frac{24 \text{ people}}{6 \text{ cars}}$; 4 people per car

10. 65 mi per 3 gal

$\frac{65 \text{ mi}}{3 \text{ gal}}$; 21.67 mi per gal

11. $49 for 5 CDs

$\frac{\$49}{5 \text{ CDs}}$; $9.80 per CD

12. $20 per dozen tarts

$\frac{\$20}{12 \text{ tarts}}$; $1.67 per tart

For Exercises 13–14, use the figure at the right.

13. Find the ratio of unshaded sections to shaded sections. Then write three equivalent ratios.

2 to 4; possible answers: 1:2, 4:8, 6:12

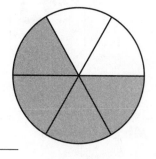

14. Find the ratio of shaded sections to all the sections. Then write three equivalent ratios.

4 to 6; possible answers: 2:3, 8:12, 12:18

Find the missing term that makes the ratios equivalent.

15. $\frac{3}{7}, \frac{\blacksquare}{14}$ ___6___

16. 7 to 5, ■ to 15 ___21___

17. 15:5, 3:■ ___1___

Mixed Review

Find the quotient. Write the answer in simplest form.

18. $\frac{7}{8} \div \frac{3}{4}$ ___$1\frac{1}{6}$___

19. $\frac{2}{3} \div \frac{1}{5}$ ___$3\frac{1}{3}$___

20. $5 \div \frac{1}{4}$ ___20___

21. $2\frac{1}{2} \div \frac{3}{8}$ ___$6\frac{2}{3}$___

Compare the fractions. Write $<$, $>$, or $=$ for each $\bigcirc$.

22. $\frac{2}{3} \bigcirc > \frac{1}{3}$

23. $\frac{5}{8} \bigcirc < 0.75$

24. $0.34 \bigcirc < 1$

25. $0.25 \bigcirc = \frac{1}{4}$

Algebra: Solve Proportions

Solve the proportion.

1. $\dfrac{8}{12} = \dfrac{x}{9}$

_____ *x = 6* _____

2. $\dfrac{2}{3} = \dfrac{16}{y}$

_____ *y = 24* _____

3. $\dfrac{7}{n} = \dfrac{21}{24}$

_____ *n = 8* _____

4. $\dfrac{a}{15} = \dfrac{3}{5}$

_____ *a = 9* _____

5. $\dfrac{4}{5} = \dfrac{12}{r}$

_____ *r = 15* _____

6. $\dfrac{m}{27} = \dfrac{4}{9}$

_____ *m = 12* _____

7. $\dfrac{7}{3} = \dfrac{c}{18}$

_____ *c = 42* _____

8. $\dfrac{20}{k} = \dfrac{4}{3}$

_____ *k = 15* _____

9. $\dfrac{35}{25} = \dfrac{7}{v}$

_____ *v = 5* _____

10. $\dfrac{10}{16} = \dfrac{z}{8}$

_____ *z = 5* _____

11. $\dfrac{30}{20} = \dfrac{9}{w}$

_____ *w = 6* _____

12. $\dfrac{e}{12} = \dfrac{25}{3}$

_____ *e = 100* _____

13. A recipe for cookies calls for 4 eggs. The recipe makes 6 dozen cookies. How many eggs would be needed to make 21 dozen cookies?

_____ *14 eggs* _____

Mixed Review

Find the circumference of the circle. Use 3.14 for π.

14. $r = 4$ in.

_____ *25.12 in.* _____

15. $r = 9$ cm

_____ *56.52 cm* _____

16. $d = 13$ ft

_____ *40.82 ft* _____

Find the area of the circle. Use 3.14 for π.

17. $r = 3$ m

_____ *28.26 m²* _____

18. $r = 8$ in.

_____ *200.96 in.²* _____

19. $d = 12$ yd

_____ *113.04 yd²* _____

Algebra: Ratios and Similar Figures

Name the corresponding sides and angles. Write the ratio of the
corresponding sides in simplest form.

1.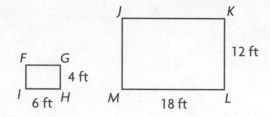

2.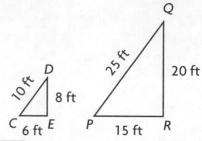

FG corresponds to *JK*; *GH* corre-
sponds to *KL*; *HI* corresponds to *LM*;
IF corresponds to *MJ*; ∠*F* corre-
sponds to ∠*J*; ∠*G* corresponds to
∠*K*; ∠*H* corresponds to ∠*L*;
∠*I* corresponds to ∠*M*; $\frac{1}{3}$ or $\frac{3}{1}$

CD corresponds to *PQ*; *DE*
corresponds to *QR*; *EC* corresponds
to *RP*; ∠*C* corresponds to ∠*P*; ∠*D*
corresponds to ∠*Q*; ∠*E* corresponds
to ∠*R*; $\frac{2}{5}$ or $\frac{5}{2}$

Tell whether the figures in each pair are similar. Write *yes* or *no*. If
you write *no*, explain.

3.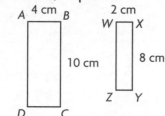

No; ratios are not equivalent.

4.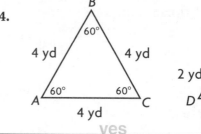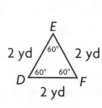

yes

The figures in each pair are similar. Find the missing measures.

5. 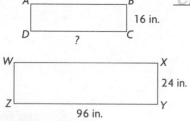   *CD* = 64 in.

6.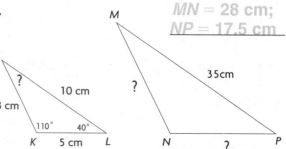

∠*J* = 30°;
MN = 28 cm;
NP = 17.5 cm

Mixed Review

Write the mixed number as a fraction.

7. $7\frac{2}{3}$ __23/3__

8. $2\frac{8}{9}$ __26/9__

9. $10\frac{1}{6}$ __61/6__

10. $5\frac{4}{5}$ __29/5__

Solve.

11. $6x = 30$ __5__

12. $48 = 8k$ __6__

13. $3.6s = 14.4$ __4__

14. $243 = 9b$ __27__

PW106 Practice

© Harcourt

Algebra: Proportions and Similar Figures

The figures in each pair are similar. Write a proportion. Then find the unknown length.

1.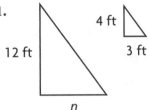

12 ft   4 ft   3 ft   n

$\frac{3}{n} = \frac{4}{12}$; $n = 9$ ft

2.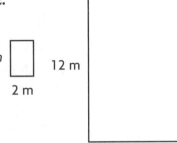

n   12 m   2 m   8 m

$\frac{n}{12} = \frac{2}{8}$; $n = 3$ m

3.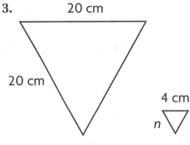

20 cm   20 cm   4 cm   n

$\frac{n}{20} = \frac{4}{20}$; $n = 4$ cm

4.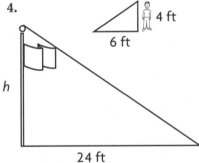

4 ft   6 ft   h   24 ft

$\frac{4}{h} = \frac{6}{24}$; $h = 16$ ft

5.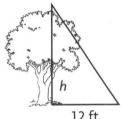

h   12 ft   3 ft   2 ft

$\frac{3}{h} = \frac{2}{12}$; $h = 18$ ft

6.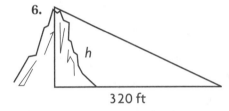

h   320 ft   5 ft   10 ft

$\frac{5}{h} = \frac{10}{320}$; $h = 160$ ft

Mixed Review

Solve and check.

7. $n + 5.5 = 23.1$

$n = 17.6$

8. $4\frac{1}{2} = k + \frac{3}{4}$

$k = 3\frac{3}{4}$

9. $28 + w = 104$

$w = 76$

Find the LCM of each pair of numbers.

10. 4, 15 ___60___

11. 7, 9 ___63___

12. 6, 16 ___48___

13. 12, 25 ___300___

Name _____

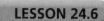

Algebra: Scale Drawings

Find the unknown length.

1. scale: 1 in.:8 ft
   drawing length: 3 in.

   actual length: __24__ ft

2. scale: 1 in.:3 ft

   drawing length: __4__ in.
   actual length: 12 ft

3. scale: 1 cm = 15 km

   drawing length: __9__ cm
   actual length: 135 km

4. scale: 4 cm = 1 mm
   drawing length: 1 cm

   actual length: __0.25__ mm

5. scale: 1 mm:12 m
   drawing length: 9 mm

   actual length: __108__ m

6. scale: 5 in.:35 yd

   drawing length: __1__ in.
   actual length: 7 yd

7. scale: 3 cm = 10 km

   drawing length: __19.5__ cm
   actual length: 65 km

8. scale: 8 cm = 3 mm
   drawing length: 4 cm

   actual length: __1.5__ mm

9. scale: 10 in.:88 yd
   drawing length: 2 in.

   actual length: __$17\frac{3}{5}$__ yd

10. scale: 1 in.:12 ft

    drawing length: __12__ in.
    actual length: 144 ft

11. scale: 1 mm = 25 m

    drawing length: __14__ mm
    actual length: 350 m

12. scale: 1 cm = 3 km
    drawing length: 15 cm

    actual length: __45__ km

Mixed Review

Find the measure of the missing angle and classify the triangle.

13.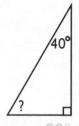

_____50°; right_____

14.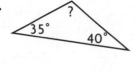

_____105°; obtuse_____

15.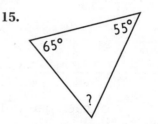

_____60°; acute_____

Simplify the expression. Then evaluate the expression for $x = 5$.

16. $10x + x^2 - 7 - 8x$

_____28_____

17. $5x + 15 + 3x - 2$

_____53_____

18. $59 + 7x - 6 + 4x$

_____108_____

Algebra: Maps

The map distance is given. Find the actual distance. The scale is
1 in. = 20 mi.

1. 4 in.

_____80 mi_____

2. 20 in.

_____400 mi_____

3. $1\frac{1}{2}$ in.

_____30 mi_____

4. 6 in.

_____120 mi_____

5. 18 in.

_____360 mi_____

6. $2\frac{1}{2}$ in.

_____50 mi_____

7. $3\frac{1}{2}$ in.

_____70 mi_____

8. $5\frac{1}{2}$ in.

_____110 mi_____

The actual distance is given. Find the map distance. The scale is
1 in. = 20 mi.

9. 250 mi

_____$12\frac{1}{2}$ in._____

10. 100 mi

_____5 in._____

11. 150 mi

_____$7\frac{1}{2}$ in._____

12. 170 mi

_____$8\frac{1}{2}$ in._____

13. 500 mi

_____25 in._____

14. 190 mi

_____$9\frac{1}{2}$ in._____

15. 220 mi

_____11 in._____

16. 580 mi

_____29 in._____

Mixed Review

Find the mean, median, and mode.

17. 27, 19, 24, 29, 18, 25, 29, 23, 28

_____$24\frac{2}{3}$; 25; 29_____

18. 39, 51, 45, 69, 22, 41, 33, 57, 30

_____43; 41; no mode_____

19. 99, 102, 97, 110, 97, 93, 98, 104, 108

_____100.9; 99; 97_____

Place the decimal point in the product.

20. $27.95 \times 4.3 = 120185$

_____120.185_____

21. $7.16 \times 1.82 = 130312$

_____13.0312_____

22. $2.709 \times 0.356 = 964404$

_____0.964404_____

© Harcourt

Percent

Write the percent that is shaded.

1.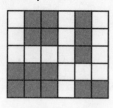

_____ 50% _____

2.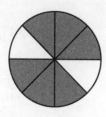

_____ 75% _____

3.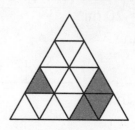

_____ 25% _____

4.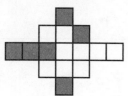

_____ 40% _____

5.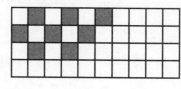

_____ 20% _____

6.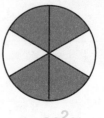

$66\frac{2}{3}$%

Write as a percent.

7. $\frac{87}{100}$ _87%_ **8.** $\frac{6}{25}$ _24%_ **9.** $\frac{9}{10}$ _90%_ **10.** $\frac{120}{100}$ _120%_

11. $\frac{13}{20}$ _65%_ **12.** $\frac{1}{10}$ _10%_ **13.** $\frac{7}{25}$ _28%_ **14.** $\frac{85}{50}$ _170%_

Compare. Write $<$, $>$, or $=$.

15. 2.3% __<__ 23% **16.** 10% __>__ 7% **17.** 5% __>__ 0.5%

18. 0.79% __<__ 7.9% **19.** 125% __>__ 12.5% **20.** 8.00% __=__ 8%

Mixed Review

Write the ratio in fraction form. Then find the unit rate.

21. 120 swimmers for 6 lifeguards ___$\frac{120}{6}$; 20 swimmers per lifeguard___

22. 385 miles in 7 hours ___$\frac{385}{7}$; 55 mi per hr___

23. \$1.92 for 8 oz ___$\frac{1.92}{8}$; \$0.24 per oz___

24. \$5.40 for a dozen muffins ___$\frac{5.4}{12}$; \$0.45 per muffin___

Write the prime factorization in exponent form.

25. 63 ___$3^2 \times 7$___ **26.** 144 ___$3^2 \times 2^4$___ **27.** 230 ___$2 \times 5 \times 23$___

Percents, Decimals, and Fractions

Write as a percent.

1. 0.7 _70%_   **2.** 0.18 _18%_   **3.** 0.84 _84%_   **4.** 0.41 _41%_

5. $\frac{3}{5}$ _60%_   **6.** $\frac{17}{100}$ _17%_   **7.** $\frac{5}{8}$ _62.5%_   **8.** $\frac{8}{25}$ _32%_

Write each percent as a fraction or mixed number in simplest form.

9. 75% _$\frac{3}{4}$_   **10.** 30% _$\frac{3}{10}$_   **11.** 55% _$\frac{11}{20}$_   **12.** 240% _$2\frac{2}{5}$_

13. 6% _$\frac{3}{50}$_   **14.** 56% _$\frac{14}{25}$_   **15.** 105% _$1\frac{1}{20}$_   **16.** $12\frac{1}{2}$% _$\frac{1}{8}$_

Write each percent as a decimal.

17. 37% _0.37_   **18.** 9% _0.09_   **19.** 0.05% _0.0005_   **20.** 321% _3.21_

Compare. Write $<$, $>$, or $=$.

21. $\frac{1}{8}$ _>_ 8%   **22.** 23% _<_ 2.3   **23.** 30% _<_ $\frac{1}{3}$

Mixed Review

Find the quotient. Write the answer in simplest form.

24. $5 \div \frac{3}{8}$ **25.** $6\frac{1}{3} \div \frac{2}{5}$ **26.** $1\frac{1}{2} \div 3\frac{1}{3}$ **27.** $2\frac{3}{5} \div \frac{1}{8}$

$13\frac{1}{3}$ _$15\frac{5}{6}$_   _$\frac{9}{20}$_   _$20\frac{4}{5}$_

For 28–30, use the figure at the right.

28. Name two angles adjacent to ∠JOK.

∠POJ, ∠KOL

29. Name an angle vertical to ∠KOL.

∠NOP

30. Name two angles supplementary to ∠MON.

∠KOM, ∠NOJ

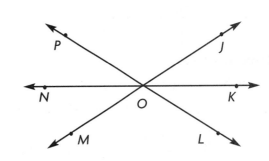

Estimate and Find Percent of a Number

Use a fraction in simplest form to find the percent of the number.

1. 10% of 8

$\dfrac{4}{5}$
_____

2. 25% of 60

15
_____

3. 50% of 50

25
_____

4. 70% of 90

63
_____

5. 80% of 70

56
_____

Use a decimal to find the percent of the number.

6. 15% of 8

1.2
_____

7. 35% of 45

15.75
_____

8. 55% of 92

50.6
_____

9. 82% of 70

57.4
_____

10. 93% of 24

22.32
_____

Use the method of your choice to find the percent of the number.

11. 52% of 40

20.8
_____

12. 96% of 84

80.64
_____

13. 81% of 34

27.54
_____

14. 12% of 300

36
_____

15. 67% of 200

134
_____

16. 4.5% of 90

4.05
_____

17. 110% of 30

33
_____

18. 140% of 100

140
_____

19. 200% of 250

500
_____

20. 400% of 80

320
_____

Estimate a 15% tip for each amount. Possible answers are given.

21. $12.00

$1.80
_____

22. $5.50

$0.85
_____

23. $23.75

$3.60
_____

24. $39.50

$6.00
_____

25. $94.80

$15.00
_____

Each proportion shows a percent and a ratio involving n.
What is the percent? What is n?

26. $\dfrac{20}{100} = \dfrac{n}{40}$

20%; 8
_____

27. $\dfrac{5}{100} = \dfrac{n}{30}$

5%; 1.5
_____

28. $\dfrac{n}{150} = \dfrac{12}{100}$

12%; 18
_____

Mixed Review

Solve and check.

29. $5n = 45$

$n = 9$
_____

30. $\dfrac{m}{3} = 12$

$m = 36$
_____

31. $99 = 9k$

$k = 11$
_____

32. $21.4 = \dfrac{a}{6.3}$

$a = 134.82$
_____

Find the sum or difference. Write the answer in simplest form.

33. $\dfrac{5}{8} - \dfrac{1}{4}$

$\dfrac{3}{8}$
_____

34. $\dfrac{2}{5} + \dfrac{1}{3}$

$\dfrac{11}{15}$
_____

35. $\dfrac{5}{7} - \dfrac{1}{3}$

$\dfrac{8}{21}$
_____

36. $\dfrac{3}{4} + \dfrac{1}{10}$

$\dfrac{17}{20}$
_____

© Harcourt

Name _____

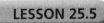

Discount and Sales Tax

Find the sale price.

1. regular price:
$18.50

| Discount
20% |

___$14.80___

2. regular price:
$35.00

| 25% off |

___$26.25___

3. regular price:
$45.50

| SAVE 50% |

___$22.75___

4. regular price:
$23.60

| SALE
80% off |

___$4.72___

5. regular price $79.50
discount rate: 15%

___$67.58___

6. regular price $153.99
discount rate: 10%

___$138.59___

7. regular price $750.00
discount rate: 18%

___$615.00___

Find the regular price.

8. sale price $47.60
discount rate: 30%

___$68.00___

9. sale price $24.70
discount rate: 5%

___$26.00___

10. sale price $239.20
discount rate: 20%

___$299.00___

Find the sales tax for the given price. Round to the nearest cent.

11. $30.00
tax: 8%

___$2.40___

12. $15.80
tax: 11%

___$1.74___

13. $654.00
tax: 7.5%

___$49.05___

14. $1,842.00
tax: 4%

___$73.68___

Find the total cost of the purchase. Round to the nearest cent.

15. price: $79.50
tax: 8%

___$85.86___

16. price: $129.95
tax: 6%

___$137.75___

17. price: $405.00
tax: 9%

___$441.45___

18. price: $3,385.00
tax: 5.5%

___$3,571.18___

Mixed Review

Complete.

19. $\frac{3}{4} = \frac{15}{20}$

20. $\frac{4}{6} = \frac{12}{18}$

21. $\frac{2}{3} = \frac{16}{24}$

22. $\frac{6}{8} = \frac{30}{40}$

Compare the fractions. Write $<$, $>$, or $=$.

23. $\frac{2}{3}$ $<$ $\frac{6}{8}$

24. $\frac{10}{12}$ $>$ $\frac{5}{8}$

25. $\frac{2}{7}$ $<$ $\frac{3}{5}$

26. $\frac{8}{9}$ $<$ $\frac{13}{14}$

© Harcourt

Simple Interest

Find the simple interest.

1. principal: $8,000
   rate: 5%
   time: 3 years

   _____$1,200_____

2. principal: $1,500
   rate: 7.2%
   time: 10 years

   _____$1,080_____

3. principal: $22,500
   rate: 4.8%
   time: 13 years

   _____$14,040_____

Find the simple interest.

	Principal	Yearly Rate	Interest for 1 Year	Interest for 2 Years
4.	$80	3%	$2.40	$4.80
5.	$150	4.5%	$6.75	$13.50
6.	$340	6%	$20.40	$40.80
7.	$600	5.2%	$31.20	$62.40
8.	$1,400	7.9%	$110.60	$221.20
9.	$5,500	9%	$495.00	$990.00
10.	$7,500	8.5%	$637.50	$1,275.00
11.	$10,000	9.6%	$960.00	$1,920.00
12.	$11,350	9.8%	$1,112.30	$2,224.60
13.	$12,975	9.5%	$1,232.63	$2,465.25

Mixed Review

Convert the temperature to degrees Fahrenheit. Write the answer as a decimal.

14. 50°C

   _____122°F_____

15. 10°C

   _____50°F_____

16. 93°C

   _____199.4°F_____

17. 23°C

   _____73.4°F_____

18. 35°C

   _____95°F_____

Use a proportion to convert to the given unit.

19. 23 wk = __161__ days

20. 42 ft = __14__ yd

21. 7 lb = __112__ oz

22. 17 gal = __68__ qt

23. 54 in. = __$4\frac{1}{2}$__ ft

24. 8 qt = __16__ pt

25. 40 cm = __400__ mm

26. 2,160 min = __36__ hr

27. 200 m = __0.2__ km

Theoretical Probability

Use the spinner at the right to find each probability. Write each answer as a fraction, a decimal, and a percent.

1. P(*M*) $\frac{1}{4}$, 0.25, 25%

2. P(*H*) $\frac{1}{8}$, 0.125, 12.5%

3. P(*J*) $\frac{0}{8}$, 0, 0%

4. P(*T*) $\frac{3}{8}$, 0.375, 37.5%

5. P(*A*) $\frac{1}{4}$, 0.25, 25%

6. P(*M* or *A*) $\frac{1}{2}$, 0.5, 50%

7. P(*T* or *H*) $\frac{1}{2}$, 0.5, 50%

8. P(*M*, *A*, or *T*) $\frac{7}{8}$, 0.875, 87.5%

A bag contains 5 blue, 3 red, and 2 green pencils. You choose one pencil without looking. Find each probability.

9. P(pink) $\frac{0}{10}$

10. P(blue) $\frac{1}{2}$

11. P(green) $\frac{1}{5}$

12. P(blue or red) $\frac{4}{5}$

Cards numbered 2, 2, 2, 3, 4, 4, 5, and 5 are placed in a box. You choose one card without looking. Compare the probabilities. Write <, >, or = in each ◯.

13. P(2) $\boxed{>}$ P(4)

14. P(4) $\boxed{=}$ P(5)

15. P(3 or 5) $\boxed{<}$ P(2, 3, or 5)

For 16–18, use the figure at the right. Find each probability.

16. P(shaded square) $\frac{5}{12}$

17. P(striped or white square) $\frac{7}{12}$

18. P(shaded or striped square) $\frac{17}{24}$

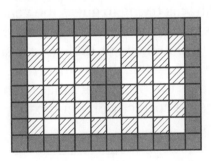

Mixed Review

Evaluate the expression for *x* = 1, 2, and 3.

19. $3x + 5$

8, 11, 14

20. $4x - x^2$

3, 4, 3

21. $7(2x + 1)$

21, 35, 49

22. $x^2(6 - x)$

5, 16, 27

Write the fraction as a percent.

23. $\frac{3}{4}$ 75%

24. $\frac{3}{10}$ 30%

25. $\frac{2}{25}$ 8%

26. $\frac{6}{5}$ 120%

Problem Solving Skill: Too Much or Too Little Information

Write if each problem has *too much, too little,* or *the right amount* of information. Then solve the problem if possible, or describe the information needed to solve it.

1. It costs $1 to buy a drink from a machine. The machine has water, 3 types of juice, and 5 different sodas. If Caryn pushes one of the buttons without looking, what is the probability that she will get one of the juices?

   too much; $\frac{1}{3}$

2. Manny is in line at the Multiplex Theater. Of all the movies playing, there are 3 that Manny wants to see. If he buys a ticket without asking for a particular movie, what is the probability that he will get a ticket for a movie he wants to see?

   too little; need number of movies playing

3. Mr. Irving is playing a game at a charity carnival. He pays $15 for a chance to play. To find out what he has won, he reaches into a bag containing a $1 bill, a $5 bill, a $10 bill, a $20 bill, and a $50 bill. What is the probability that Mr. Irving will win more than the game cost?

   the right amount; $\frac{2}{5}$

4. Jessie ordered several books from an on-line store. When they arrived, she opened the carton, examined both science fiction books and the other novels. If she then randomly chose a book to read, what is the probability she chose one of the science fiction books?

   too little; need number of other books

5. Leah was trying to guess the year Ali was born. She knew it was anywhere from 1980 through 1985. Her first guess was 1982. It was incorrect. What is the probability that Leah guessed correctly on her next try?

   the right amount; $\frac{1}{5}$

6. Albert paid $8.95 for an almanac. He found out that in his city it rains an average of 75 days each year and snows an average of 15 days each year. What is the ratio of rainy days to snowy days?

   too much; 5 to 1

Mixed Review

Use a decimal to find the percent of the number.

7. 20% of 15

   3

8. 45% of 50

   22.5

9. 90% of 70

   63

10. 65% of 30

    19.5

Find the area of each circle to the nearest whole number.

11. $r = 17$ in

    907 in^2

12. $r = 21$ cm

    1,385 cm^2

13. $d = 38$ ft

    1,134 ft^2

14. $d = 16$ yd

    201 yd^2

© Harcourt

Odds

Use the spinner at the right to find the odds in favor of the pointer landing on the given number. Write the answer in three different ways.

1. 1

2:6, 2 to 6, $\frac{2}{6}$

2. 2

3:5, 3 to 5, $\frac{3}{5}$

3. 4

1:7, 1 to 7, $\frac{1}{7}$

4. 3

2:6, 2 to 6, $\frac{2}{6}$

5. 1 or 3

4:4, 4 to 4, $\frac{4}{4}$

6. an even number

4:4, 4 to 4, $\frac{4}{4}$

Use the spinner at the right to find the odds against the pointer landing on the given letter. Write the answer in three different ways.

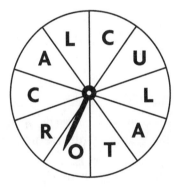

7. C

8:2, 8 to 2, $\frac{8}{2}$

8. T

9:1, 9 to 1, $\frac{9}{1}$

9. L or R

7:3, 7 to 3, $\frac{7}{3}$

10. vowel

6:4, 6 to 4, $\frac{6}{4}$

11. U

9:1, 9 to 1, $\frac{9}{1}$

12. T or a vowel

5:5, 5 to 5, $\frac{5}{5}$

Mixed Review

Write each decimal as a percent.

13. 0.75

75%

14. 0.3

30%

15. 1.06

106%

16. 0.028

2.8%

Write each percent as a decimal.

17. 8%

0.08

18. 90%

0.9

19. 20.5%

0.205

20. 340%

3.4

Experimental Probability

Adam tossed a coin 50 times. For Exercises 1–2, use the table at the right to find the experimental probability. Write the answer as a fraction and as a decimal.

Coin	Heads	Tails
Toss	22	28

1. P(Heads) $\frac{11}{25}$, 0.44

2. P(Tails) $\frac{14}{25}$, 0.56

3. What is the theoretical probability of getting heads? $\frac{1}{2}$, 0.50

Sarah rolled a number cube numbered 1 to 6. The table below shows the results of rolling the cube 50 times. Use the results in the table to find the experimental probability. Write the answer as a fraction and as a decimal.

Number	1	2	3	4	5	6
Times rolled	6	11	5	10	16	2

4. P(3) $\frac{1}{10}$, 0.10

5. P(4 or 5) $\frac{13}{25}$, 0.52

6. P(1 or 2) $\frac{17}{50}$, 0.34

7. P(5) $\frac{8}{25}$, 0.32

8. P(1) $\frac{3}{25}$, 0.12

9. P(6) $\frac{1}{25}$, 0.04

10. P(1 or 3) $\frac{11}{50}$, 0.22

11. P(3 or 6) $\frac{7}{50}$, 0.14

12. P(not 4) $\frac{4}{5}$, 0.80

13. What is the theoretical probability for each number? $\frac{1}{6}$, $0.1\overline{6}$

14. For which numbers on the number cube is the theoretical probability greater than the experimental probability? 1, 3, 6

Mixed Review

Multiply. Write the answer in simplest form.

15. $\frac{3}{4} \times \frac{2}{3}$ $\frac{1}{2}$

16. $\frac{1}{2} \times \frac{5}{6}$ $\frac{5}{12}$

17. $\frac{3}{8} \times \frac{4}{9}$ $\frac{1}{6}$

18. $\frac{5}{12} \times \frac{3}{10}$ $\frac{1}{8}$

Find the sum or difference. Write the answer in simplest form.

19. $1\frac{1}{2} + 3\frac{3}{8}$ $4\frac{7}{8}$

20. $5\frac{7}{8} - 2\frac{1}{4}$ $3\frac{5}{8}$

21. $\frac{7}{9} + 3\frac{2}{3}$ $4\frac{4}{9}$

22. $4\frac{2}{5} - 1\frac{3}{10}$ $3\frac{1}{10}$

23. $6\frac{1}{6} + 7\frac{3}{4}$ $13\frac{11}{12}$

24. $8\frac{5}{12} - 3\frac{1}{3}$ $5\frac{1}{12}$

PW118 Practice

Problem Solving Strategy: Make an Organized List

Solve the problem by making an organized list.

1. Mr. Perez is planning a trip. He can leave on Monday, Wednesday, or Friday, at 8:00 A.M., 10:30 A.M., 2:00 P.M., or 4:30 P.M. How many choices does Mr. Perez have?

_____ 12 different choices _____

2. Len is going on vacation. He has 1 jacket, 2 sweaters, and 4 shirts. How many different outfits can Len make if each outfit consists of a jacket, sweater, and shirt?

_____ 8 different outfits _____

3. Ben is having an ice cream sundae party to celebrate his birthday. He is going to have vanilla, chocolate, and strawberry ice cream and hot fudge, caramel, and marshmallow toppings. How many different sundaes will his guests be able to make?

_____ 9 different sundaes _____

4. Twelve members of the science club are planning their next field trip. They can take the trip in May or June. They can visit a science museum, bird sanctuary, zoo, or planetarium. How many different field trips involving 1 place and 1 month are possible?

_____ 8 different field trips _____

5. The 14 members of the bicycle team do not like wearing the same uniform all the time. They each purchased 2 different pair of shorts and 5 different shirts. How many different uniforms does the team have?

_____ 10 different uniforms _____

6. Nina found jackets in blue, green, and red. She found scarves in yellow, beige, and navy. She wants to buy a jacket and scarf. How many different outfits can she choose from?

_____ 9 different outfits _____

Mixed Review

A number cube is labeled 2, 3, 5, 8, 9, 9. Find each probability.

7. $P(5)$ $\dfrac{1}{6}$

8. $P(9)$ $\dfrac{1}{3}$

9. $P(\text{even})$ $\dfrac{1}{3}$

10. $P(\text{not }9)$ $\dfrac{2}{3}$

Write a proportion. Then find the unknown length. The figures are similar.

11.

3.8 yd

n

1.8 yd

5.4 yd

$n = 11.4$ yd

12.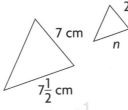

$2\frac{1}{3}$ cm

7 cm

n

$7\frac{1}{2}$ cm

$n = 2\frac{1}{2}$ cm

13.

n

60.9 m

11 m

8.7 m

$n = 77$ m

Name _____

Compound Events

Draw a tree diagram or make a table to find the number of possible outcomes for each situation. Check students' diagrams or tables.

1. spinning a pointer on a spinner labeled 1 to 4 and tossing a coin

_____ 8 outcomes _____

2. a choice of 3 cards, 2 envelopes, and 2 stickers

_____ 12 outcomes _____

3. a choice of either a red, blue, or green shirt and a black, gray, or brown jacket

_____ 9 outcomes _____

4. a choice of 4 sandwiches, 2 drinks, and 2 desserts

_____ 16 outcomes _____

Use the Fundamental Counting Principle to find the number of possible outcomes for each situation.

5. a choice of 3 juices, 2 muffins, and 3 sandwiches

_____ 18 outcomes _____

6. a choice of 3 beverages, 2 snacks, and 4 sandwiches

_____ 24 outcomes _____

7. tossing a coin and rolling 2 number cubes labeled 1 to 6.

_____ 72 outcomes _____

8. a choice of 4 shirts, 4 ties, 3 trousers, and 3 belts

_____ 144 outcomes _____

9. A Chinese restaurant offers 25 main dishes, 3 kinds of rice, and 3 different beverages. If the restaurant is open every day of the year, is it possible to eat a different meal there every day for a year? Explain.

no; $25 \times 3 \times 3 = 225$ and $225 < 365$

10. Mr. Samson is building a house. It will be in either New Jersey or New York. He wants either a one-story or a two-story house with either 3 or 4 bedrooms. How many choices does he have?

_____ 8 choices _____

Mixed Review

Write each percent as a decimal.

11. 28% __0.28__   12. 5% __0.05__   13. 163% __1.63__   14. 91% __0.91__

Find the measure of the third angle of the triangle and classify the triangle.

15. $\angle 1 = 36°$; $\angle 2 = 18°$
$\angle 3 = $ ■°

_____ 126°; obtuse _____

16. $\angle 1 = 53°$; $\angle 2 = 37°$
$\angle 3 = $ ■°

_____ 90°; right _____

17. $\angle 1 = 68°$; $\angle 2 = 59°$
$\angle 3 = $ ■°

_____ 53°; acute _____

Permutations and Combinations

Tell whether the selection is a permutation or combination

1. selecting ingredients for a tossed salad you are going to make

   _____ combination _____

2. selecting who will run first, second, third, and fourth in a relay race

   _____ permutation _____

3. selecting the batting order for a team of baseball players

   _____ permutation _____

4. selecting 4 cards from a deck of cards

   _____ combination _____

Solve.

5. How many different 2-color bows can you make from 4 different-colored ribbons?

   _____ 6 bows _____

6. In how many different ways can 5 students sit in a row with 5 desks?

   _____ 120 ways _____

7. David has 6 different plants. He wants to put 3 of them on the windowsill. In how many different ways can he select the plants to put on the windowsill?

   _____ 120 ways _____

8. In how many different ways can four people stand in line?

   _____ 24 ways _____

Mixed Review

Write each decimal as a percent.

9. 0.29 ___ 29% ___   10. 1.832 ___ 183.2% ___   11. 0.0045 ___ 0.45% ___   12. 9.6 ___ 960% ___

Find the percent of the number.

13. 64% of 50

   ___ 32 ___

14. 25% of 96

   ___ 24 ___

15. 80% of 75

   ___ 60 ___

16. 5% of 200

   ___ 10 ___

17. 12% of 48

   ___ 5.76 ___

18. 54% of 90

   ___ 48.6 ___

19. 33% of 62

   ___ 20.46 ___

20. 6% of 35

   ___ 2.1 ___

© Harcourt

Independent and Dependent Events

Write *independent* or *dependent* to describe the events.

1. roll two number cubes two times

2. select a lettered tile from a box, do not replace it, select another tile

_____ independent _____

_____ dependent _____

3. select a coin from a jar, do not replace it, select another coin

4. select a marble from a bag, replace it, select another marble

_____ dependent _____

_____ independent _____

Without looking, you take a card out of a jar and replace it before selecting again. Find the probability of each event. Then find the probability assuming the card is not replaced after each selection.

5. P(5, 6)

$$\frac{2}{25}, \frac{1}{10}$$

6. P(6, 8)

$$\frac{1}{25}, \frac{1}{20}$$

7. P(5, 7 or 8)

$$\frac{4}{25}, \frac{1}{5}$$

8. P(6, not 5)

$$\frac{3}{25}, \frac{1}{10}$$

9. P(6, 7 or 8)

$$\frac{2}{25}, \frac{1}{10}$$

10. P(5, even)

$$\frac{4}{25}, \frac{1}{5}$$

11. P(7, 7)

$$\frac{1}{25}, 0$$

12. P(7, 6, 5)

$$\frac{2}{125}, \frac{1}{30}$$

13. P(6, odd)

$$\frac{3}{25}, \frac{3}{20}$$

14. P(5, 8, 5)

$$\frac{4}{125}, \frac{1}{30}$$

15. P(5, 6, 7)

$$\frac{2}{125}, \frac{1}{30}$$

16. P(5, 5)

$$\frac{4}{25}, \frac{1}{10}$$

Mixed Review

Use the formula $d = rt$ to complete.

17. $d = 858$ cm
$r = 55$ cm per second
$t = \blacksquare$ sec

_____ 15.6 sec _____

18. $r = 48$ mi per hr
$t = 6.5$ hr
$d = \blacksquare$ mi

_____ 312 mi _____

19. $d = 423$ m
$t = 18$ min
$r = \blacksquare$ m per min

_____ 23.5 m per min _____

Write the fraction in simplest form.

20. $\frac{25}{150}$ $\frac{1}{6}$

21. $\frac{42}{210}$ $\frac{1}{5}$

22. $\frac{27}{72}$ $\frac{3}{8}$

23. $\frac{39}{52}$ $\frac{3}{4}$

PW122 Practice

© Harcourt

Make Predictions

The results of a survey of 600 randomly selected teenagers in California indicate that 150 of them use their computers at least 2 hr a day.

1. What is the probability that a randomly selected teenager in California uses the computer at least 2 hr a day?

$$\frac{1}{4}, 0.25, \text{ or } 25\%$$

2. Out of 5,500 California teenagers, predict about how many would indicate that they use their computers at least 2 hr a day.

about 1,375 teenagers

3. In a sample of 800 bicycles, the quality control department found that 32 of them were defective. If the company manufactures 8,000 bicycles, about how many of them will be defective?

about 320 bicycles

4. In a sample of 700 phones, the quality control department found that 21 of them were defective. If the company manufactures 14,000 phones, about how many of them will be defective?

about 420 phones

Use Data For 5–6, use the table. The table shows the favorite sports indicated by a random sample of 150 sixth graders from Glenville Middle School.

5. If there are 360 sixth graders at Glenville Middle School, about how many will prefer baseball? soccer?

about 108 sixth graders, about 60 sixth graders

Favorite Sports

Sport	Number of Students
baseball	45
basketball	20
soccer	25
hockey	10
track	15
football	35

6. If there are 450 sixth graders at Glenville Middle School, about how many will prefer a sport other than baseball?

about 315 sixth graders

Mixed Review

Find the value.

7. 2^4 ___16___   **8.** 5^3 ___125___   **9.** 3^3 ___27___   **10.** 1^5 ___1___

Find the LCM of each pair of numbers.

11. 5, 13 ___65___   **12.** 12, 18 ___36___   **13.** 9, 15 ___45___   **14.** 8, 22 ___88___

Understand Integers

Vocabulary

Complete.

1. _____Integers_____ include all whole numbers and their opposites.

2. The _____absolute value_____ of an integer is its distance from 0.

Write an integer to represent each situation.

3. earning 7 dollars

_____+7_____

4. digging a hole 2 feet deep

_____⁻2_____

5. taking 10 steps backward

_____⁻10_____

6. climbing up a mountain 20 feet

_____+20_____

Find the absolute value.

7. $|^-3|$ 8. $|^+3|$ 9. $|^-2|$ 10. $|^-6|$ 11. $|^+9|$ 12. $|^-15|$

___3___   ___3___   ___2___   ___6___   ___9___   ___15___

13. $|^-32|$ 14. $|^+32|$ 15. $|^-47|$ 16. $|^+78|$ 17. $|^-180|$ 18. $|^+574|$

___32___   ___32___   ___47___   ___78___   ___180___   ___574___

Write the opposite integer.

19. $^-5$ 20. $^+13$ 21. $^+21$ 22. $^-19$ 23. $^-25$ 24. $^+37$

___+5___   ___⁻13___   ___⁻21___   ___+19___   ___+25___   ___⁻37___

Mixed Review

Multiply. Write the answer in simplest form.

25. $\frac{1}{5} \times \frac{6}{7}$

___$\frac{6}{35}$___

26. $\frac{4}{9} \times \frac{3}{5}$

___$\frac{4}{15}$___

27. $\frac{4}{5} \times 30$

___24___

28. $2\frac{7}{10} \times \frac{2}{3}$

___$\frac{9}{5}$, or $1\frac{4}{5}$___

29. $3\frac{3}{4} \times 2\frac{2}{5}$

___9___

30. $1\frac{1}{2} \times 3\frac{1}{3}$

___5___

Name _____

Rational Numbers

Use the number line to find a rational number between the two given
numbers. Possible answers are given.

2 ⟵⊢⊢⊢⊢⊢⊢⊢⊢⊢⊢⊢⊢⊢⊢⊢⟶
2    $2\frac{1}{2}$ 3 $3\frac{1}{2}$ 4

1. 2 and $2\frac{1}{2}$ **2.** $2\frac{1}{2}$ and 3   **3.** 3 and $3\frac{1}{2}$ **4.** $3\frac{1}{2}$ and 4

___2.3___   ___2.8___   ___3.4___   ___3.7___

Find a rational number between the two given numbers. Possible answers are given.

5. $\frac{3}{8}$ and $\frac{4}{6}$ **6.** $\frac{3}{8}$ and $\frac{2}{3}$ **7.** $1\frac{7}{8}$ and $1\frac{3}{4}$ **8.** $^-3$ and $^-3\frac{1}{2}$

$\frac{11}{24}$ $\frac{1}{2}$ $1\frac{13}{16}$ $^-3\frac{1}{4}$

9. 3.1 and 3.2   **10.** $^-1.7$ and $^-1.8$ **11.** $^-5.6$ and $^-5.7$ **12.** 3.04 and 3.05

___3.15___   ___$^-1.72$___   ___$^-5.68$___   ___3.041___

Write each rational number in the form $\frac{a}{b}$. Possible answers are given.

13. $3\frac{1}{2}$ **14.** 0.3   **15.** 0.45   **16.** 11.2   **17.** $2\frac{1}{4}$ **18.** 3.15

$\frac{7}{2}$ $\frac{3}{10}$ $\frac{45}{100}$, or $\frac{9}{20}$ $\frac{112}{10}$, or $\frac{56}{5}$ $\frac{9}{4}$ $\frac{315}{100}$, or $\frac{63}{20}$

19. 15   **20.** 27   **21.** $3\frac{1}{5}$ **22.** 0.59   **23.** 370   **24.** $4\frac{1}{7}$

$\frac{15}{1}$ $\frac{27}{1}$ $\frac{16}{5}$ $\frac{59}{100}$ $\frac{370}{1}$ $\frac{29}{7}$

Use the Venn diagram at the right to determine
in which set or sets the number belongs.

25. 1.8   **26.** $5\frac{2}{3}$ **27.** 48

___R___   ___R___   ___all___

Rational Numbers
Integers
Whole Numbers

Mixed Review

Write the reciprocal of the number.

28. $\frac{6}{7}$ ___$\frac{7}{6}$___   **29.** $1\frac{4}{7}$ ___$\frac{7}{11}$___   **30.** 12 ___$\frac{1}{12}$___   **31.** $1\frac{1}{7}$ ___$\frac{7}{8}$___

Find the quotient. Write the answer in simplest form.

32. $\frac{2}{5} \div \frac{1}{3}$ ___$1\frac{1}{5}$___   **33.** $6 \div \frac{8}{9}$ ___$6\frac{3}{4}$___   **34.** $3\frac{3}{8} \div 1\frac{4}{5}$ ___$1\frac{7}{8}$___

Compare and Order Rational Numbers

Compare. Write < or > for ◯.

1. 0.25 ◯ 0.4

____<____

2. $\frac{3}{8}$ ◯ 0.2

____>____

3. $^-2\frac{1}{5}$ ◯ $^-2.3$

____>____

4. $\frac{^-5}{8}$ ◯ $\frac{^-3}{10}$

____<____

5. 5 ◯ $^-2$

____>____

6. $\frac{^-7}{10}$ ◯ $\frac{4}{5}$

____<____

7. $^-2.6$ ◯ $^-2.62$

____>____

8. $\frac{3}{4}$ ◯ $\frac{5}{6}$

____<____

9. $3.8 + 2.2$ ◯ $2\frac{1}{6} + 3\frac{4}{5}$

____>____

10. $3\frac{1}{2} \times 2$ ◯ $4\frac{1}{3} + 2.8$

____<____

11. $7\frac{1}{4} + 3\frac{1}{3}$ ◯ $1\frac{5}{6} \times 6$

____<____

Order the rational numbers from least to greatest.

12. $2.9, ^-1.7, \frac{9}{3}, \frac{3}{4}$

$^-1.7; \frac{3}{4}; 2.9; \frac{9}{3}$

13. $\frac{^-1}{5}, \frac{1}{9}, \frac{1}{10}, ^-0.1$

$\frac{^-1}{5}; ^-0.1; \frac{1}{10}; \frac{1}{9}$

14. $0, 0.8, ^-1.4, ^-0.6, \frac{3}{5}$

$^-1.4; ^-0.6; 0; \frac{3}{5}; 0.8$

15. $8.7, ^-9.2, ^-7.3, 6.2, 6\frac{1}{2}, 8\frac{7}{8}$

$^-9.2; ^-7.3; 6.2; 6\frac{1}{2}; 8.7; 8\frac{7}{8}$

16. $4\frac{1}{4}, 4\frac{3}{5}, 4.9, 4.08, 0.49$

$0.49; 4.08; 4\frac{1}{4}; 4\frac{3}{5}; 4.9$

Order the rational numbers from greatest to least.

17. $7.3, 6, \frac{7}{8}, 2$

$7.3; 6; 2; \frac{7}{8}$

18. $2.4, ^-1.4, ^-3, 4.7, 3.8$

$4.7; 3.8; 2.4; ^-1.4; ^-3$

19. $\frac{2}{5}, \frac{1}{10}, 0.5, ^-0.6, 0.42$

$0.5; 0.42; \frac{2}{5}; \frac{1}{10}; ^-0.6$

Mixed Review

Find the LCM of each set of numbers.

20. 4, 10

____20____

21. 7, 12

____84____

22. 8, 18, 24

____72____

23. 5, 15, 20

____60____

Find the GCF of each set of numbers.

24. 12, 20

____4____

25. 16, 42

____2____

26. 15, 50, 75

____5____

27. 36, 54, 72

____18____

Find a pair of numbers for each set of conditions. Possible answers are given.

28. The LCM is 30. The GCF is 2.

_____6 and 10_____

29. The LCM is 36. The GCF is 6.

_____12 and 18_____

© Harcourt

PW126 Practice

Name _____

Problem Solving Strategy: Use Logical Reasoning

Solve the problems by using logical reasoning.

1. Tamara, Alex, Elena, and Fred entered their dogs in the county dog show. The dogs were a terrier, a setter, a golden retriever, and a Great Dane. Neither girl owned the Great Dane. Neither boy entered a setter. Tamara owns a golden retriever. What breed of dog did Elena enter in the show?

_____ setter _____

2. Bobby, Ken, Sam, and Ayesha each participate in one sport at school. They play softball, football, basketball, and soccer. Ayesha plays first base. Ken does not play football. If Sam plays soccer, what sport does Bobby participate in?

_____ football _____

3. Adel, James, Erica, and An were comparing how far they live from school. An lives only $\frac{1}{3}$ as far as Adel. James lives twice as far as Erica and 4 times as far as An. If Adel lives 9 blocks from school, how far away does Erica live?

_____ Erica: 6 blocks _____

4. Ahmed looked over his math homework problems. He saw that $\frac{1}{2}$ of the problems were about fractions, $\frac{1}{3}$ were about decimals, and the rest were about geometry. If there were 4 geometry problems, how many problems did he have in all?

_____ 24 homework problems _____

5. Robert, Stanley, and Keith are brothers. Robert is 4 years younger than Stanley. Keith is 3 years older than Robert. Robert is 9 years older than his cousin Richard. If Richard is 11, how old is each brother?

_____ Robert: 20; Keith: 23; Stanley 24 _____

6. Adam, Carin, Dana, and Juanita are lined up for a photograph. As the photographer looks at them, Juanita is to the right of Carin. Adam is on one end. Dana is between Carin and Adam. Give their order from left to right.

_____ Adam, Dana, Carin, Juanita _____

Mixed Review

Determine whether each number is divisible by 2, 3, 4, 5, 6, 8, 9, or 10.

7. 125   8. 336   9. 1,010   10. 249   11. 9,072

____5____   __2, 3, 4, 6, 8__   __2, 5, 10__   ____3____   __2, 3, 4, 6, 8, 9__

Multiply. Write the answer in simplest form.

12. $\frac{1}{2} \times \frac{2}{5}$ 13. $\frac{3}{5} \times \frac{1}{3}$ 14. $\frac{5}{6} \times \frac{1}{4}$ 15. $\frac{3}{4} \times \frac{5}{6}$

$\frac{1}{5}$ $\frac{1}{5}$ $\frac{5}{24}$ $\frac{5}{8}$

Add Integers

Write the addition problem modeled on the number line.

1.
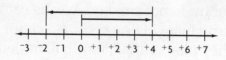

$$^+4 + {}^-6 = {}^-2$$

2.
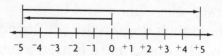

$$^-5 + {}^+10 = {}^+5$$

3.
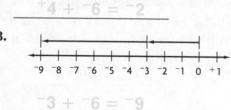

$$^-3 + {}^-6 = {}^-9$$

4.
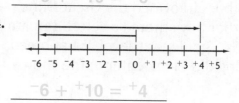

$$^-6 + {}^+10 = {}^+4$$

Find the sum.

5. $^-8 + {}^-5$
$$^-13$$

6. $^+14 + {}^-9$
$$^+5$$

7. $^-20 + {}^-4$
$$^-24$$

8. $^+31 + {}^-12$
$$^+19$$

9. $^-14 + {}^-16$
$$^-30$$

10. $^+35 + {}^+17$
$$^+52$$

11. $^-23 + {}^-9$
$$^-32$$

12. $^+39 + {}^-15$
$$^+24$$

13. $^-59 + {}^-22$
$$^-81$$

14. $^+47 + {}^-33$
$$^+14$$

15. $^-37 + {}^-26$
$$^-63$$

16. $^+49 + {}^-20$
$$^+29$$

17. $^-19 + {}^-42$
$$^-61$$

18. $^+17 + {}^-12$
$$^+5$$

19. $^+44 + {}^-17$
$$^+27$$

20. $^-64 + {}^-38$
$$^-102$$

21. $^-23 + {}^+50$
$$^+27$$

22. $^-31 + {}^-43$
$$^-74$$

23. $^+85 + {}^-15$
$$^+70$$

24. $^-59 + {}^-21$
$$^-80$$

Mixed Review

Write the opposite of each number.

25. $^-12$ $\quad ^+12$

26. $^+81$ $\quad ^-81$

27. $^-54$ $\quad ^+54$

28. $^-17$ $\quad ^+17$

Find the absolute value.

29. $|{}^-45|$ $\quad 45$

30. $|{}^+101|$ $\quad 101$

31. $|{}^+310|$ $\quad 310$

32. $|{}^-287|$ $\quad 287$

Write each rational number in the form $\frac{a}{b}$. Possible answers are given.

33. $6\frac{7}{10}$ $\quad \frac{67}{10}$

34. $^-9\frac{1}{8}$ $\quad \frac{^-73}{8}$

35. $^-1.59$ $\quad \frac{^-159}{100}$

36. 4.03 $\quad \frac{403}{100}$

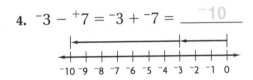
Subtract Integers

Use the number line to find the difference.

1. $^-6 - {}^-9 = {}^-6 + {}^+9 =$ ___$^+3$___

   $^-7\ ^-6\ ^-5\ ^-4\ ^-3\ ^-2\ ^-1\ 0\ ^+1\ ^+2\ ^+3$

2. $^-4 - {}^+5 = {}^-4 + {}^-5 =$ ___$^-9$___

   $^-10\ ^-9\ ^-8\ ^-7\ ^-6\ ^-5\ ^-4\ ^-3\ ^-2\ ^-1\ 0$

3. $^-6 - {}^+5 = {}^-6 + {}^-5 =$ ___$^-11$___

   $^-12\ ^-11\ ^-10\ ^-9\ ^-8\ ^-7\ ^-6\ ^-5\ ^-4\ ^-3\ ^-2\ ^-1\ 0$

4. $^-3 - {}^+7 = {}^-3 + {}^-7 =$ ___$^-10$___

   $^-10\ ^-9\ ^-8\ ^-7\ ^-6\ ^-5\ ^-4\ ^-3\ ^-2\ ^-1\ 0$

Find the difference.

5. $^+8 - {}^-9$ 6. $^-14 - {}^-6$ 7. $^+12 - {}^-9$ 8. $^+6 - {}^-2$

   ___$^+17$___   ___$^-8$___   ___$^+21$___   ___$^+8$___

9. $^+10 - {}^-3$ 10. $^+11 - {}^-9$ 11. $^-14 - {}^-7$ 12. $^-9 - {}^+3$

   ___$^+13$___   ___$^+20$___   ___$^-7$___   ___$^-12$___

13. $^-11 - {}^-9$ 14. $^-9 - {}^+4$ 15. $^-13 - {}^+5$ 16. $^-13 - {}^+2$

   ___$^-2$___   ___$^-13$___   ___$^-18$___   ___$^-15$___

17. $^-19 - {}^+7$ 18. $^+16 - {}^+12$ 19. $^+17 - {}^-11$ 20. $^-18 - {}^-9$

   ___$^-26$___   ___$^+4$___   ___$^+28$___   ___$^-9$___

21. $^+15 - {}^-14$ 22. $^-19 - {}^+13$ 23. $^-21 - {}^+6$ 24. $^-20 - {}^-8$

   ___$^+29$___   ___$^-32$___   ___$^-27$___   ___$^-12$___

Mixed Review

Find a rational number between the two given numbers. Possible answers are given.

25. 8.3 and 8.26   26. $^-4\frac{1}{2}$ and $^-4\frac{1}{3}$ 27. $^-\frac{3}{8}$ and $^-0.4$ 28. $^-1.9$ and $^-1\frac{3}{4}$

   ___8.28___   ___$^-4\frac{5}{12}$___   ___$^-0.38$___   ___$^-1\frac{7}{8}$___

Compare. Write $<$ or $>$ for each ●.

29. $\frac{2}{3}$ ● $\frac{4}{5}$ 30. $^-1.4$ ● $^-1\frac{3}{8}$ 31. $\frac{3}{4}$ ● 0.7 32. $^-5.5$ ● $^-5.6$

   ___$<$___   ___$<$___   ___$>$___   ___$>$___

Multiply and Divide Integers

Find the product or quotient.

1. ⁻3 × 7

    ⁻21

2. 8 × ⁻3

    ⁻24

3. ⁻14 ÷ ⁻2

    7

4. 24 ÷ ⁻3

    ⁻8

5. ⁻150 ÷ 25

    ⁻6

6. 36 ÷ 9

    4

7. ⁻80 ÷ ⁻4

    20

8. 75 ÷ ⁻25

    ⁻3

9. ⁻130 ÷ ⁻5

    26

10. ⁻4 × 6

    ⁻24

11. 9 × ⁻6

    ⁻54

12. ⁻6 × ⁻7

    42

13. ⁻12 × ⁻2

    24

14. 90 ÷ ⁻5

    ⁻18

15. 160 ÷ 16

    10

16. ⁻88 ÷ 11

    ⁻8

17. 42 ÷ 3

    14

18. ⁻70 ÷ ⁻7

    10

19. ⁻4 × 25

    ⁻100

20. ⁻35 × ⁻2

    70

21. ⁻5 × 12

    ⁻60

22. ⁻14 × ⁻7

    98

23. ⁻200 ÷ ⁻40

    5

24. 11 × ⁻11

    ⁻121

ALGEBRA Solve and check.

25. ⁻4y = ⁻16

    y = 4

26. $\frac{y}{-8} = 5$

    y = ⁻40

27. ⁻6y = 60

    y = ⁻10

28. $\frac{y}{-3} = ⁻3$

    y = 9

29. ⁻12y = 12

    y = ⁻1

30. $\frac{y}{-3} = ⁻9$

    y = 27

Mixed Review

Find the sum or difference.

31. ⁻2 + ⁻13

    ⁻15

32. ⁻16 − ⁻2

    ⁻14

33. ⁻3 − 24

    ⁻27

34. ⁻5 + 10

    5

Write the mixed number as a fraction.

35. $3\frac{2}{5}$

    $\frac{17}{5}$

36. $5\frac{2}{9}$

    $\frac{47}{9}$

37. $1\frac{8}{11}$

    $\frac{19}{11}$

38. $9\frac{3}{8}$

    $\frac{75}{8}$

39. $4\frac{1}{4}$

    $\frac{17}{4}$

Explore Operations with Rational Numbers

Find the sum or difference. Estimate to check.

1. $^-4.1 + 6$

1.9

2. $8\frac{1}{5} - ^-3\frac{1}{2}$

$11\frac{7}{10}$

3. $^-1\frac{7}{10} + ^-2\frac{3}{5}$

$^-4\frac{3}{10}$

4. $6.7 - ^-2.6$

9.3

5. $^-1\frac{5}{6} + 2\frac{2}{3}$

$\frac{5}{6}$

6. $12.7 + ^-3.1$

9.6

7. $^-8.4 - ^-4.8$

$^-3.6$

8. $^-2\frac{4}{5} - 3\frac{3}{5}$

$^-6\frac{2}{5}$

Find the product or quotient. Estimate to check.

9. $^-1\frac{3}{8} \div \frac{^-3}{4}$

$1\frac{5}{6}$

10. $^-4.4 \times 3.3$

$^-14.52$

11. $4\frac{1}{2} \times \frac{^-5}{6}$

$^-3\frac{3}{4}$

12. $^-0.8 \times ^-1.7$

1.36

13. $^-2\frac{1}{2} \div \frac{5}{8}$

$^-4$

14. $9.4 \div ^-5$

$^-1.88$

15. $^-1\frac{4}{5} \times ^-2\frac{2}{3}$

$4\frac{4}{5}$

16. $3.2 \div ^-2.5$

$^-1.28$

Evaluate the expression.

17. $2^3 - (^-1\frac{1}{3} + 4)$

$5\frac{1}{3}$, or $\frac{16}{3}$

18. $9.5 + (^-1.8 \times 0.2)$

9.14

19. $^-4 - ^-2 + (\frac{1}{2} \times 6)$

1

ALGEBRA Evaluate the expression for $x = ^-1.6$.

20. $^-1.4 + (x - 0.5)$

$^-3.5$

21. $^-12.5 + x$

$^-14.1$

22. $x + 3.8$

2.2

Mixed Review

Find the greatest common factor.

23. 42, 60

6

24. 20, 36

4

25. 55, 99

11

26. 48, 84

12

27. 95, 133

19

Find the mean.

28. 12, 15, 18, 14, 20, 13, 17, 11

15

29. 50, 72, 67, 55, 75, 61, 66, 58

63

30. 94, 78, 90, 83, 88, 95, 96, 80

88

31. 10, 79, 19, 56, 34, 89, 62, 27

47

Graph on the Coordinate Plane

Write the ordered pair for each point on the
coordinate plane.

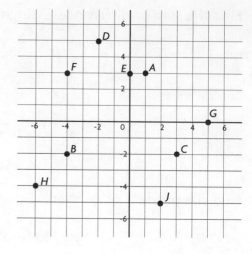

1. point A **2.** point B **3.** point C

___(1,3)___   ___($^-$4,$^-$2)___   ___(3,$^-$2)___

4. point D **5.** point E **6.** point F

___($^-$2,5)___   ___(0,3)___   ___($^-$4,3)___

7. point G **8.** point H **9.** point J

___(5,0)___   ___($^-$6,$^-$4)___   ___(2,$^-$5)___

Use the coordinate plane above. Identify the points
located in the given quadrant.

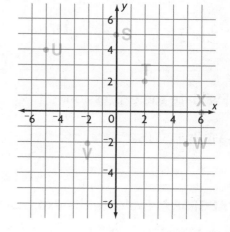

10. I ___A___   **11.** II ___D, F___

12. III ___B, H___   **13.** IV ___C, J___   Check
students'
Plot the points on the coordinate plane.   graphs.

14. S (0,5)   **15.** T (2,2)   **16.** U ($^-$5,4)

17. V ($^-$2,$^-$2)   **18.** W (5,$^-$2)   **19.** X (6,0)

Mixed Review

Find the percent of the number.

20. 78% of 152   **21.** 12% of 37   **22.** 57% of 238   **23.** 0.6% of 200

___118.56___   ___4.44___   ___135.66___   ___1.2___

Find the circumference of each circle. Use 3.14 for π.

24. $r = 7$ in   **25.** $d = 12$ ft   **26.** $d = 15$ m   **27.** $r = 30$ cm

___43.96 in___   ___37.68 ft___   ___47.1 m___   ___188.4 cm___

Graph Functions

Complete the function table.

1.

x	1	2	3	4	5
y	3	4	5	6	7

2.

x	1	2	3	4	5
y	5	10	15	20	25

3. Graph the data from Exercise 1 on the coordinate plane.

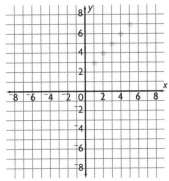

4. Graph the data from Exercise 2 on the coordinate plane.

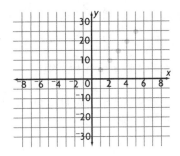

5. Write an equation relating y to x for the data in Exercise 1.

 $y = x + 2$

6. Write an equation relating y to x for the data in Exercise 2.

 $y = 5x$

7. Use the equation $y = x - 5$ to make a function table. Use the integers from ⁻3 to 3 as values of x. Then use words and a graph to show how x and y are related.

x	⁻3	⁻2	⁻1	0	1	2	3
y	⁻8	⁻7	⁻6	⁻5	⁻4	⁻3	⁻2

Check students' graphs. Possible answer: Subtract 5 from x to find the value of y.

Mixed Review

Find the number of possible outcomes for each situation.

8. 5 flavors of ice cream and 4 toppings

___20 choices___

9. 4 shirts, 6 ties, and 2 jackets

___48 choices___

10. 3 kinds of pancakes and 4 kinds of syrup

___12 choices___

Evaluate the expression for $n = ⁻3, ⁻1,$ and 4.

11. $3n - 2(n + 5) + n$

___⁻16, ⁻12, ⁻2___

12. $5 + 2n - (6 + n)$

___⁻4, ⁻2, 3___

Problem Solving Skill: Make Generalizations

Solve by making a generalization.

Anita uses 2.5 c of flour to make a dozen muffins. The table shows the number of dozens of muffins made, x, for different amounts of flour, y.

x (doz)	2	4	6	8	10
y (c)	5	10	15	20	25

1. What equation can be used to show the amount of flour that Anita uses? D

   A $y = x - 2.5$ C $y = x + 2.5$

   B $y = x \div 2.5$ D $y = 2.5x$

2. How much flour does Anita use to make 16 dozen muffins? J

   F 6.4 c   H 20 c

   G 18.5 c   J 40 c

Anita charges $0.75 for each muffin.

3. Write an equation to show the cost, m, when Anita sells n muffins.

   $m = 0.75n$

4. How much will Anita charge for 15 muffins?

   $11.25

Rick spends $8 on supplies for his dog-grooming business. The table shows his profit, y, for several income amounts, x.

x	$30	$35	$40	$45
y	$22	$27	$32	$37

5. What equation can be used to show Rick's profit? B

   A $y = 8 - x$ C $y = \frac{1}{8}x$

   B $y = x - 8$ D $y = x + 8$

6. How much profit did Rick make if he earned $105? J

   F $113   H $101

   G $109   J $97

Rick charges $35 for a regular dog grooming.

7. What equation can Rick use to show the amount that he earns, y, when he grooms x dogs?

   $y = 35x$

8. How much will Rick earn if he grooms 12 dogs?

   $420

Mixed Review

Find the simple interest.

9. principal: $2,200
   rate: 7.3%
   time: 4 yr

   $642.40

10. principal: $14,000
    rate: 6.7%
    time: 8 yr

    $7,504

11. principal: $35,000
    rate: 8.2%
    time: 12 yr

    $34,440

© Harcourt

PW134   Practice

Name _____

Graph Transformations

Transform the figure according to the directions given.
Name the new coordinates.

1.

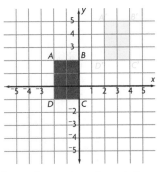

Translate 4 units right
and 3 units up.

$A'(2,5)$, $B'(4,5)$,

$C'(4,2)$, $D'(2,2)$

2.

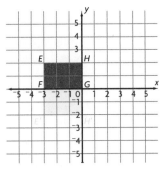

Reflect across the
x-axis.

$E'(^-3,^-2)$, $F'(^-3,0)$,

$G'(0,0)$, $H'(0,^-2)$

3.

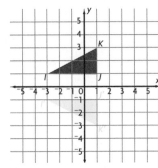

Reflect across the
x-axis.

$I'(^-3,^-1)$, $J'(1,^-1)$,

$K'(1,^-3)$

Rotate the figure around the origin according to the directions given.
Name the new coordinates.

4. 90° clockwise

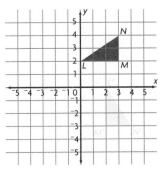

$L'(2,0)$, $M'(2,^-3)$,

$N'(4,^-3)$

5. 180° counterclockwise

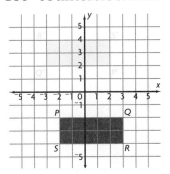

$P'(2,2)$, $Q'(^-3,2)$,

$R'(^-3,4)$, $S'(2,4)$

6. 90° counterclockwise

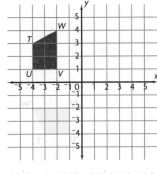

$U'(^-1,^-4)$, $V'(^-1,^-2)$,

$W'(^-4,^-2)$, $T'(^-3,^-4)$

Mixed Review

Find the next three possible terms in each sequence.

7. 4, 12, 36, 108, . . .

324; 972; 2,916

8. 27, 19, 11, 3, . . .

$^-5$, $^-13$, $^-21$

9. 7, 11, 18, 29, . . .

47, 76, 123

Solve and check.

10. $h + 12 = 37$

$h = 25$

11. $m + 8 = 19$

$m = 11$

12. $43 = 4 + p$

$p = 39$